NUTSH

LAND LAW
IN A NUTSHELL

Monica Zhao

AUSTRALIA
Law Book Co.
Sydney

CANADA and USA
Carswell
Toronto

HONG KONG
Sweet & Maxwell Asia

NEW ZEALAND
Brookers
Auckland

SINGAPORE and MALAYSIA
Sweet & Maxwell Asia
Singapore and Kuala Lumpur

NUTSHELLS

LAND LAW
IN A NUTSHELL

SIXTH EDITION

by

Michael Haley
Solicitor, Professor of Law
University of Keele

Based on the original text by
William B. Howarth

London ● Sweet & Maxwell ● 2004

First Edition 1987
Second Edition 1991
Third Edition 1994
Reprinted 1997
Fourth Edition 1997
Fifth Edition 2000
Reprinted 2001
Reprinted 2002
Reprinted 2003
Published in 2004 by
Sweet & Maxwell Limited of
100 Avenue Road, Swiss Cottage, London, NW3 3PF
http://www.sweetandmaxwell.co.uk
Typeset by
LBJ Typesetting Ltd of Kingsclere
Printed & bound by Creative Print & Design, Wales

A CIP Catalogue record
for this book is available
from the British Library

ISBN 0–421–871601

CONTENTS

1. INTRODUCTORY TOPICS

CLASSIFICATION OF PROPERTY

English law makes a primary distinction between real and personal property (realty and personalty). Although the peculiar English history of leases provides an exception, this distinction corresponds in the main to the distinction drawn in civil law systems between immovable and movable property. A modern day significance of this distinction is that real property (or proprietary) rights have the ability to bind future purchasers of the land whereas personal rights (such as a licence) do not.

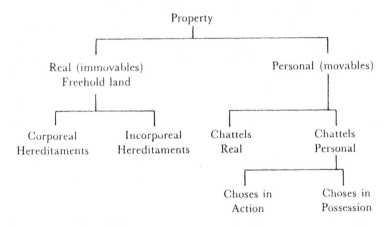

1. Real property. Originally, real property was the term applied to any property that was the subject matter of a real action in the common law courts. This applied only to freehold interests in land and was not available to actions relating to leaseholds. A distinction is also to be drawn between *corporeal hereditaments* which are inheritable things capable of being physically possessed (*i.e.* the land and buildings themselves) and *incorporeal hereditaments* which are inheritable rights in land which cannot be possessed (*e.g.* easements, profits and restrictive covenants).

2. Personal property. This relates to any property that could be made the subject of a personal action, such a personal action being against the individual rather than the property. The consequence of a personal action (for dispossession, say, of a horse) was that the wrongful dispossessor could either hand back the personal property or pay damages. With a real action, if a freeholder had been wrongly dispossessed of land then possession of the land had to be handed back.

3. Chattels real (leases). Historically, leases were treated as personal property simply because only a personal action could be taken for dispossession in the courts. A lease was, therefore, a purely contractual relationship. Accordingly, leases were treated in the same way as chattels, hence the expression "chattels real". Today, of course, a lease is a property right and is capable of being a legal estate in land.

4. Chattels personal. This category covers all other personal property and can be subdivided into choses in action and choses in possession. A *chose in action* is an intangible right (it has no physical existence) which can only be claimed or enforced by action and not by taking physical possession of the thing itself, *e.g.* a debt, cheque, bond, share certificate, patent and copyright. Such assets are, however, capable of being sold, pledged and transferred. A *chose in possession* is a tangible right that can be enjoyed by taking physical possession of the thing itself, *e.g.* a car, book, furniture and jewellery.

5. Differences and distinctions. Whether property is classified as real or personal may assume significance in a number of situations. For example:

(a) where a testator by will leaves his realty to X and his personalty to Y;
(b) a contract to dispose of personalty does not need to adhere to any prescribed form, but as regards land contracts the formalities of s.2 of the Law of Property (Miscellaneous Provisions) Act 1989 apply and the contract must be in writing, contain all express terms and be signed by both parties;
(c) the purchase price paid for land will include fixtures, but does not include personal property.

OWNERSHIP AND LAND

1. Since the Norman Conquest (1066) and the introduction of feudalism, the Crown technically owns all land in England.

Albeit convenient, it is not, therefore, strictly correct to speak of an individual "owning" land. Instead, an individual can own only an *estate* in land. The quality of that ownership will vary, of course, according to the type of estate which is owned. Ownership rights, moreover, need not be vested in the same person, *e.g.* where a trust exists or where there are a number of different estates in the same piece of land. Consequently, it is more appropriate to deal with a person's right to possession (seisin) in determining title to land.

2. In the physical sense, land includes not only the ground, soil or earth, but also all buildings on the land, any fixtures attached thereto, mines and minerals and any incorporeal rights such as easements: s.205(1)(ix) of the Law of Property Act 1925. At common law the extent of ownership is said to extend up to the sky and down to the centre of the earth (*cujus est solum, ejus est usque ad coelum et ad inferos*), but this general rule is subject to a variety of exceptions:

(a) *sudden accretions from the sea* of substantial size belong to the Crown, though gradual accretions belong to the owner;

(b) *the foreshore* (land between high and low water mark) belongs to the Crown unless otherwise specially granted;

(c) *the airspace* up to a reasonable height belongs to the owner; *Lord Bernstein of Leigh v Skyways & Geneva Ltd* (1977) and if interfered with may give rise to an action in trespass or nuisance: *Kelsen v Imperial Tobacco Co.* (1957). Under the Civil Aircraft Act 1982, no action can be taken in respect of aircraft that pass over property at a reasonable height. In *Anchor Brewhouse Developments Ltd v Berkley House (Docklands Developments) Ltd* (1987) an injunction was granted to prevent the jib of a crane swinging over adjoining property as this amounted to a trespass;

(d) *minerals* belong to the tenant at common law, but statute has considerably reduced these rights so that gold and silver in mines belong to the Crown and most valuable minerals such as coal or petroleum are similarly vested therein;

(e) *water rights* are governed by the Water Resources Act 1991. The basic rule is that a licence from the National Rivers Authority must be obtained for any extraction of water from any source, *i.e.* percolating or from a defined channel. No licence is required in the case of abstractions of small quantities of water for certain limited authorised purposes, *e.g.* domestic purposes of the occupiers household or agricultural purposes other than spray irrigation;

(f) *river beds*. The owner of land through which a non-tidal river flows owns the riverbed. Where a river separates two plots of land, each plot owner owns the bed up to the middle. Tidal rivers belong to the Crown.

Fixtures and fittings

1. "Land" includes any object that is attached to the land so as to form part of it (*quicquid plantatur solo, solo cedit*). Consequently when a chattel (*e.g.* a door or radiator) is affixed to land or to a building, it may become a fixture and thus become part of the land itself. This is of importance in deciding whether a landowner, on selling or leasing property, can remove objects from the land. The problem may also arise in connection with what property is the subject of a mortgage, devise by will or strict settlement. If a chattel has not become a fixture, it is known as a fitting. Although there is no decisive formula that can be applied by the courts, there are two general rules which help to distinguish a fixture from a chattel and these are the degree of annexation and purpose of annexation tests: *Holland v Hodgson* (1872).

2. The *degree of annexation* test. Originally, physical attachment to the land was the crucial issue. If it was attached, it was a fixture. In modern times, the emphasis has moved away from such a rigid rule and rests now upon why the item was introduced on to the land (*i.e.* the purpose test). It follows, therefore, that an item can become a fixture without any attachment to the land (*e.g.* a chalet: *Elitestone Ltd v Morris* (1997)) and can remain a chattel despite secure attachment (*e.g.* a greenhouse: *Dean v Andrews* (1985)). The degree test is not, however, redundant. First, an absence of physical attachment will (unless an item is so heavy that it does not require any attachment) usually entail that the item is a chattel. Secondly, the degree test may become significant where the purpose of annexation is unclear. In such cases, the extent and method of physical attachment can then give rise to a series of (sometimes even conflicting) evidential presumptions. For example, if the attachment is only slight the item is presumed to be a chattel (say, a free standing cooker); if removal of the item will cause

damage to the fabric of the building it is presumed to be a fixture (say, kitchen units); and if attachment is the only way in which the item can be enjoyed it is presumed to be a chattel (say, a heavy ornamental mirror). Once invoked, which ever presumption is chosen is likely to be decisive of whether an item is a fixture or not: *Hamp v Bygrave* (1983).

3. The *purpose of annexation* test. The purpose test addresses the issue of why the item was introduced on to the land. The basic question is whether the item was there in order to be a permanent improvement or was intended instead to be a temporary installation. The court here is primarily concerned with objective intentions and not the subjective intentions of the person who brought the item on to the land. The court will consider the nature of the item and the nature of its attachment to the land. Hence, some items are clearly going to be fixtures (*e.g.* bathroom fittings, kitchen units, doors and wall tiles) whereas others are clearly going to be chattels (*e.g.* lampshades, washing machines, gas fires and curtains). Fitted carpets, however, have caused some difficulties. The courts have been undecided as to whether they are to effect a permanent improvement (see *Young v Dalgety Plc* (1987) or are attached to the building merely so that they can be used (see *Botham v TSB Bank Plc* (1997). As mentioned, when the purpose is unclear, the court will resort to the degree of annexation test and the associated presumptions. Objects which form part of the architectural design of a house or grounds will be regarded as permanent fixtures whether or not they are attached. In *Re Whaley* (1908) an Elizabethan tapestry in an Elizabethan house was held to be a fixture. Similarly, in *D'Eyncourt v Gregory* (1866) freestanding ornaments were regarded as fixtures because they formed an integral part of the landscaped garden.

4. In the absence of contrary agreement, the general rule is that if an item constitutes a fixture it cannot be removed from the land. Accordingly, a vendor must leave fixtures for a purchaser and a mortgagor cannot remove fixtures during the course of the mortgage. In relation to landlord and tenant (similar rules apply also as between tenant for life and remainderman) there are limited exceptions. A tenant may remove certain "tenants fixtures" either during the lease or within a reasonable time thereafter. These include:

(i) trade fixtures (*i.e.* items attached by the tenant for the purpose of a trade or business);

    (ii) ornamental and domestic fixtures (*e.g.* blinds, stoves and grates);

    (iii) agricultural fixtures provided that an opportunity to purchase them is first given to the landlord.

Land and the European Convention on Human Rights

The Human Rights Act 1998 incorporates the Convention into English law. Article 1 of the Convention contains a guarantee of property rights by offering:

    (i) freedom from arbitrary deprivation of possessions;
    (ii) freedom from unjustified controls on the use of property;
    (iii) peaceful enjoyment of possessions.

The Convention rights bind the state, local authorities, courts and tribunals. It is also possible for them to be enforceable as between individuals. The rights are not, however, absolute and may be overridden if their disregard is warranted by domestic law and is in the wider public interest. A principle of proportionality operates here which means that there must be a balance between the interference and the furtherance of a social interest.

    Article 6 offers a right to a fair trial of, say, property disputes; Article 8 gives a right to respect for the home and family life; and Article 14 offers freedom from discrimination in the exercise of Convention rights.

---

2. THE DOCTRINE OF TENURES AND ESTATES

THE DOCTRINE OF TENURES

From the time of the Norman conquest, English land law adopted the continental system of feudalism (hierarchy dominated by a sovereign or chief and based on mutual promises of protection and military service). William the Conqueror (1066–87) regarded the whole of England as his by conquest and granted land, not by out and out transfer, but to be held of him as overlord. Persons holding land of the Crown might then grant land to another (subinfeudation) to hold of him in return for services. The feudal pyramid that was constructed was based upon the land tenure system. The tenure of the land identifying the conditions on which land was held. These varied in terms of nature and status. Tenure was the main bond holding society together, the lord protecting those who held land of him. It is now, however, largely of historical interest.

Forms of tenure

1. Free tenures. Where the nature of the duties were fixed, and the services were rendered freely. The most common types of free tenure were:

(a) *chivalry* such as knight's service (military service in return for land) and grand sergeantry (personal services for the king);
(b) *socage* which primarily involved the provision of agricultural services of a fixed nature;
(c) *spiritual* tenure such as frankalmoign and divine service, which involved grants to ecclesiastical bodies in return for the saying of prayers or masses for the repose of the soul of the lord and for his spiritual well-being.

2. Unfree tenures. Unfree tenures included *villeinage* and *copyhold* which were labour intensive services, often agricultural, but were not fixed in nature and amount. By the fourteenth century, these were commuted to payment of rent, enabling the lord to hire labour independently.

Incidents of tenure

As part of the tenure system the lord was entitled to certain incidents which were often of real value to him. These varied with the different types of tenure held. The most common incidents were:

(a) *homage, fealty and suit of court* which involved the tenant swearing to be the lord's man and to perform the feudal obligations as well as agreeing to attend the lord's court;

(b) *relief* which amounted to the payment of money to the lord when the tenant died;

(c) *aids* which were payments required when the lord needed ransom or the eldest son was knighted or his daughter needed dowry;

(d) *escheat and forfeiture* occurred where the land passed to the lord because of failure of heirs or where the tenant committed a serious crime;

(e) *wardship* which gave to the lord the right to retain profits from the land where the tenant was an infant;

(f) *marriage* which gave the lord the right to select the spouse of a tenant.

Effects of the tenure system today

In general, the doctrine of tenures has no practical effect today. The Abolition of Tenures Act 1660 and the Law of Property Act 1925 abolished almost all incidents and forms of tenure. Consequently, there is now only one form of tenure, *i.e. socage* or freehold tenure as it is usually termed. It is now assumed that a landowner holds land as tenant in chief directly from the Crown, but without the provision of services. On sale, the purchaser replaces the vendor as tenant in chief.

THE DOCTRINE OF ESTATES

Whereas the doctrine of tenures dealt with the conditions on which land was held, the doctrine of estates is concerned with the length of time for which land is held. As all land in England is held of the Crown, English law has developed the concept of the estate which has its emphasis on the right to possession (seisin). An estate represents a stake in land of defined duration and, as such, is an abstract entity which represents the extent of a person's rights to possession. Reduced to its basics, an estate reflects the quality of ownership in land.

Classification of estates

Estates vary in size according to their potential duration, the major distinction being between freehold and leasehold estates.

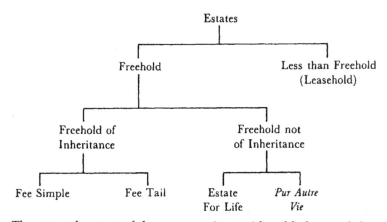

The general nature of these estates is considered below and they are also considered in further at appropriate places in the text. There are two principal categories of estate: *freehold* and *less than freehold*. A freehold estate (originally derived from the law of tenures) is one whose duration is uncertain, whereas an estate less than freehold is one for a period whose duration is fixed or capable of being fixed (*e.g.* a lease for 10 years).

Freehold estates

There are four types of freehold estate:

1. the fee simple. This is the largest estate in terms of duration and is as near to "absolute ownership" as it is possible to achieve under English law. The word "fee" connotes inheritability and "simple" indicates that right to inherit is unrestricted (*i.e.* it is inheritable by general heirs whether ascendants, descendants or collateral). The fee simple is virtually everlasting in that it continues as long as the person entitled for the time being has "heirs" left to inherit. The classic words of limitation used to create such an estate are "to X and his heirs".

2. the fee tail. This is an inheritable estate which lasts as long as the original grantee or any of his descendants live. The term "fee tail", "estate tail", "entail" or "entailed interest" are often used to describe the same estate. A classic method of creation was to use the words "to X and the heirs of his body". A restriction of the line of descendants to the male or female species only could be created by a "fee tail male' or a "fee tail female". Following the Trusts of Land and Appointment of

Trustees Act 1996, it is no longer possible to create an entailed interest.

3. the life estate. This arises where there is a grant of an estate to the grantee for his life. The estate is not inheritable and, since 1925, can only exist as an equitable estate.

4. the estate *pur autre vie.* This is a species of life estate where the right to the estate exists for the duration of someone else's life. A grant of Blackacre "to X for the duration of Y's life" would create such an estate which terminates on Y's death.

Estates less than freehold

These were admitted into the estate system in the 16th century and now comprise various forms of leasehold interest including:

(a) fixed terms of certain duration, *e.g.* "to X for 99 years";
(b) a term the duration of which is capable of being rendered certain, *e.g.* "to Y from year to year";
(c) a tenancy at will which has been described as the lowest estate known to the law.

Estates in possession, remainder and reversion

A further consequence of the concept of the "estate" is that the law allows various smaller and simultaneous estates to be carved out of the fee simple estate: *e.g.* "to A for life: B for life; C in fee simple". The following observations need to be made:

(i) an estate *in possession* is one where a present right to immediate enjoyment is given, *e.g.* there is no preceding estate to postpone enjoyment. In the preceding example the estate of A is in possession. The estate of A being in possession is known as a "particular estate";
(ii) where land will revert back to the original grantor, then the grantor has an estate *in reversion* so that if Blackacre is conveyed by X "to A for life", then the estate of X is a reversion;
(iii) in the grant "to A for life; B for life; C in fee simple", the estate of B and C are estates *in remainder*, *i.e.* they do not have a present right to actual enjoyment and their right to possession is postponed to the future.

The rights of a fee simple owner

The fee simple being the largest estate that can exist in land carries with it many of the rights which would be associated with absolute ownership of property. These include:

1. Natural rights. There is a natural right of support for land (although not for buildings which must be acquired by easement or covenant) and a natural right to an unpolluted free flow of air across property. These rights exist automatically and do not require any form of grant.

2. The right of alienation. A fee simple owner may dispose of his land in any way he chooses, either by deed or by will.

3. The right of enjoyment. The rights of enjoyment possessed by a fee simple owner are extensive. In physical terms he may enjoy everything on, beneath and above the land, but there are practical restrictions to this rule. In addition, the right of enjoyment may be compromised by the property rights of others. For example, a third party might have an easement to cross the land, a restrictive covenant to prevent building on the land or the right to occupy the land by virtue of a lease. In exercising rights over land, moreover, the fee simple owner must not interfere with the legal rights of others. Consequently liability in tort may arise:

(a) where a nuisance is caused, *e.g.* smells or noise;
(b) under the rule in *Rylands v Fletcher* (1868), *e.g.* where something brought on to the land (*e.g.* water or oil) escapes and causes damage.

4. Fishing rights. In non-tidal waters the owner has the exclusive right to fish though this right may be granted to others, *e.g.* fishing clubs. In tidal water, the public has a right to fish up to the point of ebb and flow of the tide.

5. Wild animals. Wild animals cannot form the subject matter of ownership, but a fee simple owner has a qualified right to catch, kill and appropriate. Certain species of animals and birds are, however, protected by statute, *e.g.* the Wildlife and Countryside Act 1981.

6. Statutory restrictions. Statutory restrictions have eroded away certain rights of an owner. Many of these statutes are based on public interest and illustrate public authority interference, *e.g.* the Town and Country Planning Acts; the Rent Acts; and a variety of Housing and Public Health Acts.

7. Items found on the land. A distinction is here to be drawn between lost items found on the surface of the land and items which are found under, attached to or embedded in the land. As regards surface objects, the finder has a better claim to the item unless the landowner has exerted sufficient control over the land and things which might be found on it. The finder will otherwise have a good title which can be defeated only by the true owner of the item: *Parker v British Airways Board* (1982) (bracelet found in airport lounge where no scheme for finding lost property existed). If the finder is a trespasser, however, the finder's claim is thought to be relegated also behind that of the landowner: *Waverley B.C. v Fletcher* (1995). If the item is found either under, in or attached to the land, the landowner has a better claim than the finder does. This was demonstrated in the *Waverley* case where a metal detector was used to unearth a valuable brooch in a public park owned by the local authority. The local authority had a better claim to the brooch and this was particularly so as the digging up and removal of property was not a permitted public recreational use and constituted trespass.

8. Treasure trove. Treasure trove is subject to the Treasure Act 1996. The definition of treasure includes all finds of major historical significance. When treasure is found it will usually vest in the Crown. Coroners will hold inquests to determine whether items found constitute treasure, but in most cases without a jury. The Secretary of State has produced a code of practice for dealing with rewards to finders of treasure.

---

3. LAW AND EQUITY

Because of the deficiencies of the common law as administered in early common law courts, *i.e.* delay, complicated procedures of the writ system and inadequate remedies, a body of law known as equity was developed by the Court of Chancery giving a new range of rights and remedies to assist a potential litigant. It is in the realms of property law that equity has made its greatest contribution.

Rights created by equity

1. The trust. At common law, it was not possible to have an enforceable arrangement under which one person would hold the legal title of property for the benefit of another. The common law was preoccupied with legal title only. Equity intervened to allow such an arrangement in the form of the trust (originally called a "use"). The common denominator of all trusts is that legal title (*i.e.* nominal, paper title) to the property is held by trustees whereas equitable or beneficial (substantive) ownership is vested in the beneficiary. Equity ensures that the trustees are bound to administer the trust for the benefit of the beneficiary and, if they are in default, they will personally be liable to account to the beneficiary.

2. Equitable right to redeem. This is the right of a mortgagor (borrower) to redeem the mortgage loan (by payment of capital, interest and costs) even after the legal (*i.e.* contractual) date for redemption has passed (see Ch.10).

3. Restrictive covenants. The shortcomings in the law of covenants were, in part, mitigated by equity by allowing the burden of a restrictive freehold covenant (*i.e.* a negative covenant) to run in equity and, thereby, bind future purchasers of the burdened land. This development is usually traced back to the decision in *Tulk v Moxhay* (1848) (see Ch.12).

Special remedies granted in equity

Equity developed a series of discretionary remedies (*i.e.* remedies which cannot be claimed as of right) in order to overcome the inadequacy of the common law remedy of compensation. These include:

1. Injunction. Although there are various types of injunction, the basic classification is between a mandatory injunction (which compels someone to do something) and a prohibitory injunction (which restrains someone from doing something).

2. Specific performance. This is an order of the court compelling performance of a contractual obligation in cases where damages are inappropriate.

3. Rescission. This is an order of the court canceling a contractual obligation and restoring the parties to their original (pre-contract) position.

4. Rectification. The court may order a contract to be altered (*i.e.* physically rewritten) where the contract does not accurately reflect the true intention of the parties. This most commonly occurs when a term is omitted from a written contract due to a common mistake of the parties. Rectification for a unilateral mistake can occur, but only when there has been fraud, unconscionabilty or some other sharp practice by one of the parties.

5. Certain new procedures. These were introduced by equity to ensure an effective trial process. These include the subpoena, discovery of documents and interrogatories.

Legal and equitable rights

1. A legal right is a right *in rem* (in the thing itself) which is automatically binding upon the enitre world. An equitable right, however, is a right *in personam*. Hence, it has a more limited capacity to bind third parties. It will not bind a bona fide purchaser for value of a legal estate without notice of the equitable interest ("equity's darling"). Although both are property rights, an equitable right is, traditionally, inferior to its legal counterpart.
2. In order for a right to be legal it must be listed in s.1(2) of the Law of Property Act 1925 as having that capacity (*e.g.* a mortgage or easement); it must equate with a freehold or leasehold estate (and not, say, with a life interest); and it must, as a general rule, be granted by a formal document known as a deed. For example, if A and B are adjoining landowners and B grants to A the permanent right to cross his land in order to reach a main road then A has an easement over B's land. If the easement is created by deed then it will be a legal easement. If it is created merely in writing, then it must be an equitable easement. If B sells his land to C, the purchaser will automatically be bound by a legal easement because it is a right

enforceable against all persons. If the easement is equitable, the doctrine of notice will determine whether the right binds C.

The Doctrine of Notice

The basic doctrine of notice provides that an equitable interest will bind all persons other than "equity's darling", *i.e.* the bona fide purchaser for value of the legal estate with no notice of the equitable interest, or anyone who claims through him: *Pilcher v Rawlins* (1872). The essential features of the doctrine are:

1. Bona fide. The purchase must act in good faith, *i.e.* there must be no fraud or sharp practice: *Midland Bank v Green* (1980). Usually, however, this condition merely emphasises that the purchaser must be innocent as to notice.

2. Purchaser. Includes any person who takes the property by sale, mortgage, will, lease or otherwise, but excludes any acquisition by operation of law (*e.g.* under the intestacy rules).

3. Value. Includes any consideration for money or money's worth or marriage (*i.e.* an ante-nuptial settlement of property). The consideration need not be adequate and can even be at an under value. Natural love and affection will not suffice. Inheriting under a will does not amount to value.

4. Of a legal estate. The estate purchased must be a legal estate which includes freehold, leasehold and, by virtue of statute, a mortgage. If the purchaser only acquires an equitable estate he will not, therefore, take free of prior equitable interests. In that situation, equity operates on the principle that where the equities are equal the first in time prevails.

5. Without notice. There are three types of notice: actual, constructive and imputed:

(a) *actual notice:* a purchaser has actual notice of all matters that have been brought to his attention, but not of facts that have come to his attention by way of vague rumours. Rights that are registrable in the Land Charges Register and are registered constitute actual notice: s.198 of the LPA 1925 (see Ch.4);

(b) *constructive notice:* a purchaser is expected to make reasonable enquiries before completing the transaction. If the
purchaser fails to do so, he is deemed to have "constructive notice" of all the matters that would otherwise
have been discovered: s.199 of the LPA 1925. The purchaser should make the following reasonable enquiries:

    (i) inspect the land and query anything that appears
inconsistent with the title offered by the vendor. In
Kingsnorth Finance v Tizard (1986), for example,
occupation by the seller's wife fixed the purchaser
with constructive notice of her equitable rights in the
property. This was so even thought the husband lied
and tried to hide traces of her occupation.

    (ii) investigate the seller's title to the land by trawling
through previous conveyances (title deeds) going
back at least 15 years. The purchaser is deemed to
have notice of any equitable rights recorded on the
title during that time: s.44 of the LPA 1925, as
amended.

(c) *imputed notice:* where a purchaser employs an agent, such
as a solicitor or surveyor, any notice (whether actual or
constructive) attributed to the agent is imputed to the
purchaser. In the *Kingsnorth Finance* case, the constructive
notice of an agent surveyor was imputed to the purchaser
(the mortgagee). The agent must, however, be employed
by the purchaser at the time when the actual or constructive notice is acquired: *Halifax Building Society v
Stepsky* (1997).

6. Once an equitable right is defeated by a bona fide
purchaser for value of a legal estate with no notice of the
equitable interest, it entirely loses the ability to bind third
parties. It cannot be resurrected and cannot, therefore, bind a
future purchaser even if that purchaser knows of the existence
of the right: *Wilkes v Spooner* (1911).

7. The impact and effect of the doctrine of notice has been
considerably reduced by system of land charges registration. It
does, however, retain a limited, residual role (see Ch.4). As
regards registered land, the traditional view is that the doctrine
of notice has no relevance whatsoever (*Midland Bank v Green*
(1980)).

4. ESTATES, INTERESTS AND LAND CHARGES

1. In 1925, there was a systematic overhaul of property law. A raft of legislation was passed in that year which included the Law of Property Act; the Settled Land Act; the Trustee Act; the Administration of Estates Act; the Land Charges Act (now 1972); and the Land Registration Act (now 2002).

2. The legislation achieved the following general effects:

(a) it reduced the number and effects of the tenure system;
(b) it achieved a closer approximation of land law and the law of personal property;
(c) it reduced the number of legal estates in land;
(d) it extended the system of registration of charges and registration of title;
(e) it abandoned many miscellaneous outmoded rules.

3. There are now two separate systems of conveyancing in existence:

(a) *unregistered conveyancing*: where a purchaser of property requires a vendor to prove his title through production of historic title deeds. A minimum "root of title" of 15 years is currently required;
(b) *registered conveyancing*: this is now governed by the Land Registration Act 2002. The scheme allows a purchaser to check title by reference to the Land Register which is a central register open to public inspection. This is not to be confused with the Land Charges Register.

REDUCTION OF LEGAL ESTATES AND INTERESTS

1. In an attempt to simplify conveyancing and to assist a purchaser of land, one of the principal innovations of the Law of Property Act 1925 was to reduce the number of legal estates that can exist in land. Section 1(1) provides that the only estates in land which can be legal are the fee simple absolute in possession and the term of years absolute.

2. The section further provides that there are now four interests in or over land that are capable of being legal:

(a) an easement right or privilege in or over land equivalent to an estate in fee simple absolute in possession or a term of years absolute;

(b) a rentcharge in possession issued out of or charged on land being either perpetual or for a term of years absolute;

(c) a charge by way of legal mortgage;

(d) rights of entry exercisable over or in respect of a legal term of years absolute, or annexed, for any purpose, to a legal rentcharge.

3. It follows that, if an estate or interest is not within these lists, it must necessarily be equitable: s.1(3) of the LPA 1925. For example, a life estate is an equitable estate and a restrictive covenant and a trust interest are equitable interests.

4. If within the statutory lists, the estate or interest has the potential to be legal. Whether or not it is legal, however, will usually turn upon how it was created. The general rule is that, for a legal estate or legal interest to exist, it must be created formally by deed: s.52(1) of the LPA. For example, an easement granted merely in writing can only be equitable. An exception to the rule is with leases not exceeding three years which can be legal even if granted in writing or, indeed, orally: s.54(2).

5. The difference between an "estate" and an "interest" is that an estate represents the quality of ownership (and brings with it rights to possess and deal with the land) whereas an interest is merely a right over someone else's land (*e.g.* an easement or restrictive covenant).

LEGAL ESTATES

The fee simple absolute in possession

1. As shown, the fee simple is an estate of inheritance that lasts as long as the "owner" has heirs. The word "absolute" is used to distinguish a fee simple that may continue forever from a *modified fee* of which there are three main species:

(a) determinable fee. This is a fee simple which will end automatically on the happening of a specified contingency. For example, "to X in fee simple until the church tower of St Paul's falls down" or "to X in fee simple until his bankruptcy." It is not certain that the event will ever occur;

(b) a fee simple on condition subsequent This is a fee simple which is liable to cease if a condition is broken. If the event ever occurs the grantor has a right of re-entry, but the estate does not automatically terminate. For example, "to X in fee simple on condition that the church tower on St Paul's never falls down," or "to X in fee simple, but if he becomes bankrupt then to Y absolutely";

(c) a fee simple on condition precedent. This is a fee simple which will commence on a particular event, for example, "to X and his heirs when he reaches the age of 30".

2. The difference between a determinable fee and a fee simple on condition subsequent is not easy to identify. The major distinction lies in the words used to connect the fee simple to the contingent event:

(a) whenever the words set the limit for the estate first granted, it is determinable, for example, "until", "while", "during" or "as long as";

(b) where the words form a grant subject to the possibility of it being defeated then a fee simple on condition subsequent is created, for example, "provided that", "on condition that", "if it happens that" and "but if";

(c) the importance of the distinction is that, while the determinable fee can only exist in equity behind a trust (it not being "absolute" for the purposes of s.1), it is possible for a fee simple on condition subsequent to be "absolute." The Law Property Amendment Act 1926 states that a fee simple subject to a legal or equitable right of entry or re-entry is for the purposes of the LPA 1925 absolute. Consequently, because a right of re-entry is given to a grantor, if the contingent event ever occurs under a fee simple on condition subsequent, this invokes the words of the Amendment Act and renders it a fee simple absolute.

3. If the condition attached to a *determinable* fee is rendered void, the whole grant fails. If the estate is a *conditional* fee and the condition is rendered void, this creates a fee simple absolute and only the condition is invalidated. For this reason the courts are much stricter in construing conditional fees than they are in construing determinable fees based on the same type of condition. A condition may be void because:

(a) it is too vague and a precise definition cannot be given to the terms of the condition. In *Re Jones* (1953), a condition that the donee should not have a social or other relationship with a certain named person was void for uncertainty;

(b) it prevents alienation. A provision which entirely prevents the sale of the land will be void: *Hood v Oglander* (1865). A partial restraint may, however, be valid: *Re Macleay* (1875);

(c) it purports to exclude operation of bankruptcy laws: *Re Machu* (1882);

(d) it is in total restraint of marriage. *Clayton v Ramsden* (1943). A partial restraint may be valid as in *Re Tepper's Will Trusts* (1986) where a reference to marrying outside "the Jewish faith" was a permissible condition;

(e) it is contrary to public policy. Any provision that encourages immorality, illegality, the breakdown of marriage or the family will be inoperative.

4. Land held for certain purposes (say, for use as highways or schools) is treated as being absolute even though the land will revert back to the grantor if the special purpose ceases: s.7 of the LPA. Under s.7(2) a fee simple vested in a corporate body remains absolute although it may determine on dissolution of the company.

5. A fee simple will be absolute even if incumbered, whether by mortgage, restrictive covenant or otherwise.

6. The term "in possession" in s.1(1)(a) is used to distinguish present enjoyment from future enjoyment. A grant to "A for life; remainder to B in fee simple" does not give B a legal estate. Possession includes receipt of rent and profits of land, or the right to receive them: s.205(1)(XIX) of the LPA. Hence, a fee simple owner who has leased his land remains a legal estate owner despite no longer having physical possession.

A term of years absolute

1. This is a legal estate of fixed duration and includes a lease of less than a year, or for a year or years or a fraction of a year, or from year to year: s.205(1)(XXVII) of the LPA. This includes periodic tenancies.

2. The term "absolute" here has little significance as s.205 of the LPA provides that a term of years will still be absolute even

though it may be liable to determination by notice, re-entry, operation of law, or by a provision for cesser on redemption (of mortgage) or on any other event.

3. There is no requirement that the lease should be in possession; it may commence in the future (*i.e.* this is known as a "reversionary lease"). Nevertheless, s.149 of the LPA makes most reversionary leases void if they are to take effect more than 21 years from the date of the instrument of creation).

Legal interests

Those rights which are capable of being legal interests are listed in s.1(2) of the LPA and are:

1. Easements rights and privileges. The definition will extend to cover *profits à prendre*, but not restrictive covenants. The grant must be perpetual or for a fixed term, so that a grant of an easement for life is necessarily equitable.

2. Rentcharges. A rentcharge is a right to a periodical sum of money secured on land. Note that:

(a) although the rentcharge must be "in possession", the Rentcharges Act 1977 allows rentcharges to be legal even if they are to become payable at a future time after their creation. An exception to this rule is where the rentcharge is to take effect following the determination of an earlier interest;

(b) the rentcharge must be issued out of or charged on land;

(c) the period of the rentcharge must be fixed or perpetual. This definition must now be read in the light of the Rentcharges Act 1977 which provides that:

   (i) no new rentcharge can be created after the coming into force of the Act (August 1977). "Estate rentcharges" (those that are attached to freehold land in order to ensure that the burden of positive covenants can bind future purchasers) provide an exception to this;

   (ii) existing rentcharges are to have a maximum life of 60 years calculated from the date of commencement of the rentcharge or the date the Act came into force, whichever is the later.

3. Charge by way of legal mortgage. Since the Land Registration Act 2002, this is the only method by which a legal mortgage can be created in relation to registered land. Previously, as in unregistered land, a mortgage could also be created by the grant of a term of years absolute.

4. Rights of entry. If a tenant under a legal lease fails to pay rent or to comply with other covenants in the lease, the landlord will usually reserve in the lease a right to re-enter. Similarly, if a legal rentcharge falls into arrears, the grantee has a legal right to enter to collect the money due.

Contracts to create an estate or interest in land

In addition to the normal requirements of a contract (*e.g.* offer and acceptance, an intention to create legal relations and consideration), s.2 of the Law of Property (Miscellaneous Provisions) Act 1989 provides that for a land contract to be valid it must also be in writing, contain all the express terms and be signed by both parties. This rule does not, however, apply to short leases (*i.e.* periodic tenancies and leases which do not exceed three years), contracts under the Financial Services and Markets Act 2000, and auction contracts. Similarly, s.2 does not apply to chattel contracts, contracts that have already been performed, collateral contracts, a contract to compulsory purchase property and so-called "lock out" agreements which prevent negotiation with other prospective purchasers for a specified period. Otherwise the general rule applies to contracts to grant any interest or estate in land. Examples include, the creation of either an option to purchase (*Spiro v Glencrown Properties Ltd* (1991)) or an option to surrender a lease (*Commission for the New Towns v Cooper (Great Britain) Ltd* (1995); the creation of a legal or equitable mortgage (*United Bank of Kuwait v Sahib* (1996)); and the variation of an existing land contract (*McCausland v Duncan Lawrie* (1996)).

(a) *Writing* is defined widely by the Interpretation Act 1978 and includes typing, printing, photography, lithography and other modes of representing or reproducing words in a visible form;

(b) *Signature* is also widely defined and includes any visible mark made by the contracting parties or their authorised agents which is intended to authenticate and adopt the document: *First Post Homes Ltd v Johnson* (1995).

(c) *Document* can include more than one page or piece of paper and it is possible for two documents to be joined together by express or implied reference to one another. Provided that there is this "joinder of documents" (also known as "incorporation of terms") some of the terms, can be in one document while the remainder are in another: *British Bakeries v Thorbourne Retail Parks* (1991).

(d) *Express terms* must be stipulated in the written document. Implied terms (of which there are few) need not be specified. Examples of implied terms are that vacant possession will be given and that conveyance of the property will occur within a reasonable time after contract.

(e) "Subject to contract" is a label which, when attached to a document, prevents a contract from arising, prevents one document being joined to another and, even though there might be detrimental reliance, operates as a bar to an estoppel claim: *James v Evans* (2000). The label once attached persists until abandoned either expressly or though implication.

(f) *Invalidity* is the result of a non-compliance with s.2, but this outcome can be avoided by either rectification (re-writing) of the agreement for mutual mistake; the waiver of an omitted term by the party who benefits exclusively from it; enforcing an estoppel to avoid an unconscionable outcome; or recognising the existence of a constructive trust which is outside the capture of the 1989 Act.

LAND CHARGES REGISTRATION

1. There are five registers created under the Land Charges Act 1925 (now 1972) all kept on a central computer at the Land Charges Department of the Land Registry at Plymouth. The five registers are:

(a) the register of pending actions;
(b) the register of annuities;
(c) the register of writs and orders affecting land;
(d) the register of deeds of arrangement;
(e) the land charges register.

It is with this register that the remainder of this chapter is concerned.

2. The Land Charges Act 1972 enables the registration of a land charge to protect some (but not all) interests in land. Those interests that are outside the scheme remain subject to the doctrine of notice and, as regards an interest under a trust or settlement, the overreaching machinery. Otherwise, the system of land charges has supplanted the doctrine of notice in respect of third party rights in unregistered land. Persons dealing with unregistered land are expected to make a search of the land charges register against the names of previous owners in order to discover any protected interests.

3. Land charges only concern land where the title to that land is unregistered. If the title is registered, the land is instead subject to very different provisions of the Land Registration Act 2002 (see Ch.5).

Principles of land charges registration

1. After 1925, if a third party right is registrable (*i.e.* there is a class of land charge that can protect it) its potential to bind a future purchaser of the land depends upon whether or not a land charge has been registered.

2. Registration of a land charge is deemed to constitute actual notice to all persons and for all purposes connected with the land: s.198 of the LPA 1925. Registration of a land charge will ensure that the interest binds a new purchaser.

3. A failure to protect a registrable interest by the entry of land charge will, as a general rule, make the interest void against a purchaser for value: s.4 of the LCA 1972. Where, however, the interest is either an estate contract (Civ); a charge for death duties (Di); restrictive covenant (Dii); or equitable easement (Diii) it will only be void for non-registration against a purchaser of a legal estate who gives "money or money's worth." Whether a purchaser has actual notice or not in these situations is irrelevant: s.199(1) of the LPA.

4. Land charges are registered against the name of the estate owner at the time the interest is created, not against the land. As names will get lost in the mists of time, this is a major defect of the scheme. An official search of the land charges register will be conclusive if made against the correct names of the estate owners and it provides 15 working days immunity against any subsequent entries.

Categories of land charge

1. Within the land charges register there are six classifications of land charge, although only classes C, D and F require significant attention.
2. *Class C land charges:*

   (a) **C(i)**: this protects a *puisne* (pronounced "puny") mortgage, that is, a legal mortgage not protected by deposit of title deeds. The possession of tile deeds offers ultimate protection and first priority for a lender: s.97 of the LPA 1925;

   (b) **C(ii)**: this land charge protects a limited owner's charge, that is, a financial charge on the land entered by a person who is not an absolute owner. For example, a tenant for life who pays inheritance tax out of his own pocket may protect payment in this way;

   (c) **C(iii)**: this land charge protects a general equitable charge which is not protected by title deeds. This extends to an equitable, financial charge which is not registrable under any other class, for example, an equitable mortgage, an unpaid vendor's lien, and an equitable rentcharge;

   (d) **C(iv)**: this land charge protects a contract to convey or create a legal estate. The contract must amount to a binding and enforceable agreement which means that it must satisfy the writing formalities of s.2 of the Law of Property (Miscellaneous Provisions) Act 1989. The definition covers ordinary contracts for sale, leasing or mortgaging of the legal estate, as well as a right of pre-emption (first refusal) and an option to purchase. In *Midland Bank v Green* (1980), an option to purchase which was not registered was void against a purchaser of a legal estate for money or money's worth. In *Phillips v Mobil Oil Co. Ltd* (1989), an option to renew contained in a lease, being an estate contract, was similarly void for want of registration. A request for an overriding lease under s.20(6) of the Landlord and Tenant (Covenants) Act 1995 may also be registered as a C(iv) land charge.

3. *Class D land charges*

   (a) **D(i)**: this land charge can be entered by the Inland Revenue in respect charge of unpaid inheritance tax in respect of land;

(b) **D(ii)**: this land charge protects a restrictive covenant provided that it was entered into after 1925 and was not made between a landlord and tenant. Restrictive covenants made prior to 1926 are still governed by the doctrine of notice;

(c) **D(iii)**: this land charge protects an equitable easement that was created after 1925. Rights acquired by estoppel are not within this category and are not registrable: *Ives v High* (1967). Pre-1926 equitable easements remain governed by the doctrine of notice.

4. Class F land charge

The class F land charge caters for the protection of the right of occupation given to spouses by the Family Law Act 1996. If, for example, a husband holds the legal estate as sole owner or on trust for himself and his spouse by way of co-ownership, the spouse will have the right to register a charge and protect her rights of occupation: see *Wroth v Tyler* (1974). The entry of a class F land charge can be made without the consent of the owning spouse. If the process is misused by a spouse, the court has the power to cancel the land charge: *Barnett v Hassett* (1981).

Interests outside the scheme

1. With the exception of puisne mortgages (C(i)), legal interests fall outside the land charges machinery and, therefore, remain binding *in rem* on all the world.

2. Some equitable interests are also outside the scheme and whether they will bind a purchaser will depend upon the doctrine of notice. Such interests include:

(a) restrictive covenants and equitable easements created before 1926;

(b) beneficial interests under a trust of land (such interests can, however, be overreached: see below);

(c) equitable rights of entry;

(d) equitable rights based on estoppel.

The Law of Property Act 1969

This amending Act recognised that two major problems had emerged in relation to the discovery of registered land charges and took certain steps to deal with them:

1. Hidden names. On investigating title, it is possible that the name of a previous estate owner, against whom a land charge has been entered, is not disclosed. It may be hidden behind the (minimum of 15 years) root of title. Nevertheless, the purchaser will be bound by such an undiscoverable land charge. The problem was partly addressed in s.25 of the 1969 Act which allows for such a purchaser to claim compensation from the public purse. This is, of course, provided that he did not actually know of the land charge.

2. Discovery after contract. It is usual for a land charges search to be made only after contracts have been entered, but before completion of the transaction. A land charge discovered after contract remains binding, but s.24 of the 1969 Act allows the purchaser to withdraw from the contract. This is again provided that the purchaser did not actually know of the land charge.

Overreaching

1. Only certain family interests can be overreached by a purchaser (this is a process which transfers the interest formerly in the land into the proceeds of sale of the land) and they are an interest under a strict settlement within the Settled Land Act 1925 and a beneficial interest under a trust of land. In both cases, the legal estate and beneficial interests have become separated and, historically, gave rise to two problems. First, how to make land readily marketable without the purchaser being inconvenienced by the interests of the beneficiaries? Secondly, how best to protect the interests of the beneficiaries?

2. The problem was solved by the overreaching machinery now contained in s.2 of the Law of Property Act 1925. This is a mechanism that allows the purchaser to take free of a beneficiary's interest (even if the purchaser knew of that interest) provided that the purchase money is paid to at least two trustees or a trust corporation. The latter includes the Public Trustee; a trustee in bankruptcy and a court appointed trustee corporation. The beneficiary must then look to the trustees for financial recompense. In *Williams & Glyn's Bank v Boland* (1981), a wife's equitable interest in land was not overreached on a subsequent mortgage because the mortgage money was paid only to the husband and not, as is necessary, to two trustees. The rights of the wife (as beneficial owner) bound the

purchaser. In *City of London Building Society v Flegg* (1988) there was an arrangement whereby the interests in a family property were shared by parents and their adult children. The legal estate was vested in the adult children who mortgaged the property to a building society. It was held that the mortgage lender over-reached the interests of the parents. The mortgage money was, on this occasion, paid to two trustees. The same rule applies where the property is used as security for a bank overdraft facility: *State Bank of India v Sood* (1997).

3. Under the Trusts of Land and Appointment of Trustees Act 1996 extensive changes to the way successive interests in land are created have taken place (see Chap. 7). For example, trusts for sale and the associated doctrine of conversion have been abolished; the creation of any new strict settlements has been prevented and the old system has been replaced with a new trust of land. Nevertheless, the overreaching mechanism is retained. It is arguable that the consultation provisions imposed by the 1996 Act (which require trustees to give effect to the wishes of the beneficiaries) will reduce the number of incidents of overreaching.

5. REGISTERED LAND

Introduction

The object of registration of title is to make the transfer of land simpler, quicker, cheaper and more reliable. On the conveyance of *unregistered* land, the task of the seller is to produce documentary evidence (title deeds) of past transactions going back at least 15 years. This is to establish that he is the current owner of the estate he is intending to sell. The seller is said to show a "root of title". The ambition of registered conveyancing is to do away with the onerous requirement of repeated examination of title deeds on successive sales. In its place, there is a tripartite register which provides for a purchaser a description of the land, the name of the registered proprietor, and any third party rights which are registered against the land. In this way, the purchaser should have a complete and up-to-date picture of the state of the title which, if accompanied by a search in the local land charges register, enquiries of the vendor and a physical inspection of the land, should provide adequate protection. The system, however, is not perfect in that certain rights are binding upon a purchaser even though they are not recorded on the register. The system of registered conveyancing is rapidly subsuming its unregistered counterpart and, since 1990, the whole of England and Wales has been an area of compulsory registration. This means that on the next sale or other disposition of unregistered land the title will have to be registered, *i.e.* compulsory registration will take place. The events that trigger this first registration are considered below.

The registered system has recently undergone major overhaul in the form of the Land Registration Act 2002 (in force since October 13, 2003). The changes introduced are radical and, unfortunately, complex. For example, there are different rules that apply according to whether it is a first registration or a registered disposition and there are, to make matters worse, transitional provisions that operate in the short-term to soften the full impact of the 2002 Act.

Aims of the 2002 Act

The Land Registration Act 2002 is designed to achieve a variety of purposes. The major ones are:

(a) to make all titles registered by extending the range of events which trigger compulsory first registration and allowing Crown land to be registered;

(b) to pave the way for electronic conveyancing and to make the land register capable of easy on-line investigation. Registration will take place simultaneously with the creation of estates and interests and, thereby, the current registration gap of two months will disappear;

(c) to provide more effective protection for title to land and third party rights;

(d) to ensure that the register is an accurate reflection of title by reducing the categories of overriding interest;

(e) to ensure that most express dispositions of land are noted on the register;

(f) to introduce a new system of acquiring title by adverse possession.

BASIC PRINCIPLES OF REGISTERED CONVEYANCING

It is often said that there are three fundamental principles underpinning the system of registered title:

1. The mirror principle. Which is that the register should be an accurate reflection of the current title and matters affecting the land. The 2002 Act has heightened the reflective nature of the register by reducing the number of rights that can exist off-register and increasing the number of rights that must be protected on the register in order to bind third parties. The aim is that title to land can be investigated with the bare minimum of additional enquiries. A major crack in this mirror principle concerns overriding interests (now styled "interests which override either first registration or registered dispositions") which do not appear on the register, but are automatically binding on a purchaser (see below);

2. The curtain principle. Which operates to hide any interest arising under a trust behind the curtain of registration. This means that interests that can be overreached by a purchaser (by paying the purchase money to two trustees or a trust corporation) are not detailed on the register. Instead, the existence of a trust interest might be disclosed by the entry by a beneficiary of a "restriction" on the Land Register, but this will only alert a purchaser that there is a trust interest that must be overreached;

3. The insurance principle. Which is that the state guarantees the title as declared on the register and will pay compensation to any person who suffers loss as a result of any error on the register: s.58 of the LRA 2002. Rectification and alteration of any errors on the register is, however, possible: s. 65 (see below).

The Land Register

Section 1 of the 2002 Act provides that a register of title is to be maintained by the Land Registry. The Land Registry is headed by the Chief Land Registrar. Applications for registration are dealt with by district land registries and each has its own regional catchment area. The system is largely, but as yet not completely, computerised. Since 1988, the Land Register has been open to public inspection. The register of title for individual properties is structured in three parts:

(a) *the property register* which contains a physical description of the land with reference to a plan. A legal description of the property is also included and this will note the advantageous features of the land such as any easements and restrictive covenants which exist for the benefit of the land;

(b) *the proprietorship register* which specifies the type of title that has been registered, the name and address of the proprietor and any "restrictions" entered which limit the ability of the registered proprietor to deal with the land;

(c) *the charges register* which contains entries of third party rights adversely affecting the land, *e.g.* mortgages, estoppel rights, equitable easements and restrictive covenants.

What can be registered?

There are three categories of property interest that can be registered:

1. A limited number of estates and interests in land are capable of what is often called "substantive registration" which means that they can be registered with a separate title and, thereby, each is given its own unique title number. A list of these rights is contained in s.2 of the LRA 2002. They include a fee simple absolute in possession (freehold), a term of years absolute with more than seven years left unexpired (leasehold), a profit a prendre existing in gross (*i.e.* without there being a dominant tenement), a rentcharge and a franchise (a royal privilege). The registered proprietor of such a right does not, after the 2002 Act, receive a land certificate;

2. A legal mortgage of registered land must be created by a charge expressed to be by way of legal mortgage. The charge must then be registered by the lender in the charges register relating to the mortgaged land and then becomes known as a "registered charge". It is only on registration that the mortgage takes effect as a legal charge: s.51. Mortgagees no longer obtain a charge certificate following registration;

3. Those burdens that are neither capable of being substantively registered nor are registered charges are called "registrable interests". Such interests must be protected by the agreed or unilateral entry of a notice in the charges register (s.34(2)). Unilateral notices are appropriate where the registered proprietor does not agree to the entry. On entry of the unilateral notice, the registrar will notify the registered proprietor and the latter can then apply for the notice to be cancelled. The matter can, if necessary, be referred to a character known as "the adjudicator" appointed under the 2002 Act. Interests which are to be

protected by a notice are traditionally known as "minor interests" and include most property rights, for example, certain
types of lease, equitable easements, restrictive covenants, estate
contracts, spousal rights of occupation and estoppel rights. The
general rule is that, if protected by a notice, the interest will
bind a purchaser (s.29(2) of the LRA 2002) whereas, if it is not, it
will be void for non-registration against a new registered
proprietor (s.29(1)). A number of rights cannot, however, be
protected by a notice and these include a beneficial interest
under a trust of land or Settled Land Act trust; leasehold
covenants; and leases which were granted for three years or
less: s.33.

Registered estates (ownership)

1. When land is first registered, the nature of the title described
in the proprietorship register will depend upon the proof of the
title that the estate owner can demonstrate. The guarantee
afforded will reflect the type of title that is registered and might
also differ according to whether the title is freehold or leasehold:

 (a) *absolute title*, which applies to both freehold and leasehold
 estates, is the best and most common title available. It is
 registered only when the registrar can verify that the title
 is safe and cannot be significantly challenged. In the case
 of freehold land, s.11 provides that the proprietor registered with absolute title takes subject only to
 incumbrances and other entries on the register and overriding interests (unless the contrary is stated on the
 register). In the case of leasehold land, s.12 ensures that
 registration with absolute title guarantees to the world
 that the lease was validly granted (*i.e.* that superior titles
 have been investigated and that the landlord had the
 capacity to grant the lease);
 (b) *good leasehold title*, not surprisingly, applies only to a
 leasehold estate and has no relevance to freeholds: s.10.
 This title is appropriate where the landlord's title has not
 been investigated. Otherwise, it is the same as absolute
 title: s.12(6);
 (c) *qualified title* is relevant where there is a defect in, or
 doubt as to, title which prevents registration with absolute title. For example, title might have been acquired in
 breach of trust or, on first registration, can be established

for only a limited period. Qualified title extends to both freehold and leasehold land (ss.9, 10) and is similar to absolute title except that it is subject to the potential defect;

(d) *possessory title* is applied for when, on first registration, the applicant is unable to produce any title deeds. This arises where the claim to freehold or leasehold title is based upon adverse possession (squatter's rights). Possessory title is the same as absolute title except that it does not affect or prejudice the enforcement of any counter estate or rights which existed at the time of first registration: s.12.

2. Upgrading title. Section 62 permits the registrar, either of his own volition or at the request of a person interested (usually, the registered proprietor himself), to upgrade title. If the title is freehold, either a qualified or possessory title can be upgraded to absolute title. In the case of possessory title, this regrading can occur when the title has been registered for 12 years. If title is leasehold, a qualified or possessory title can be upgraded to good leasehold title if the registrar no longer has doubts as to the validity of the lease. Any of those leasehold titles can be regraded to absolute title when the registrar is assured of the title of the landlord (*e.g.* the freeholder's title has now been registered in its own right). Any person who suffers loss because of an upgrading to a superior title can claim indemnity under the 2002 Act.

3. Failure to register. Section 6 imposes a duty to register on the transferee of a relevant estate. An application to register a freehold or leasehold title, moreover, must be made within two months of either a registered disposition or a triggering event: s.6(4). This period can be extended by the registrar if there is good cause to do so. If registration has not been applied for within this time frame, the transaction is void as to legal title and, instead, the existing registered proprietor will usually hold the legal title on trust for the transferee: s.7(2)(a). In relation to a lease/mortgage, however, the disposition takes effect as a contract to create a legal lease/mortgage (s.7(2)(b)). The danger is that the transferee (particularly a mortgagee) could lose priority to an interest created after the ineffective disposition.

First Registration

1. As unregistered land is being rapidly phased out, the 2002 Act allows for voluntary first registration of title and encourages this by offering discounted fees. Compulsory registration of what was previously legal title in unregistered land is required on the occurrence of certain triggering events. The duty to register and the sanctions of non-registration are as explained above. The transactions which operate to trigger first registration are set out in s.4 and include:

(a) the transfer of a freehold estate or an assignment of a leasehold estate (with seven years of more remaining unexpired) whether for value, by means of an assent (re a deceased's estate), by way of gift or court order. This does not include the surrender of a lease;

(b) the grant out of qualifying freehold or leasehold estate of a lease/sublease of more than seven years whether for value, by way of gift or order of the court. This does not include the surrender of a lease;

(c) the grant by a local authority of a "right to buy" lease to an existing periodic tenant under the Housing Act 1985;

(d) the creation of a reversionary tenancy which is to take effect in possession more than three months subsequent to its grant;

(e) the creation of a protected first legal mortgage of a qualifying freehold or leasehold estate. Taking out a subsequent second mortgage of unregistered land will not, therefore, trigger compulsory registration.

2. Cautions against first registration. As an application for first registration may well affect the interests of others, in certain circumstances the 2002 Act allows for those interested to lodge a caution against first registration. The effect of this is that, when the application for first registration is made, the person who entered the caution will be notified and given the opportunity to object to the registration. If such objection is made then, short of agreement, the matter must be referred to the adjudicator: s.71. A person may lodge a caution against first registration when he claims to be either the owner of a qualifying estate or entitled to an interest affecting a qualifying estate (*e.g.* matters registrable under the Land Charges Act 1972). Cautions will be noted in a register of cautions which will be maintained at the Land Registry. A caution must be entered only with reasonable cause and, if not, the landowner can apply for it to be cancelled.

Unregistered interests which override registration

1. These rights are traditionally called 'overriding interests' and bind a purchaser even though they do not appear on the registered title. The range of rights that may benefit from this special treatment have been dramatically reduced by the Land Registration Act 2002. While this simplifies the system and reinforces the "mirror principle" (see above), the Act instils some complexity by drawing a distinction between those rights which override first registration and those rights which override dispositions of land already registered. To make matters more complicated, transitional provisions operate to deal with pre-existing overriding interests.

2. Rights which override first registration. These are set out in Schedule 1 of the 2002 Act and include:

(a) legal leases of seven years or less (para.1);
(b) the interests of persons in "actual occupation" (para.2), but excluding interests under a strict settlement, the spousal right of occupation given by the Family Law Act 1996, overriding leases granted under the Landlord and Tenant (Covenants) Act 1995 and a reversionary tenancy (*i.e.* a tenancy to take effect in the future) if it is not to begin within three months of its grant. For the meaning of "actual occupation" see below. Although there is no mention here of when enquiry is made of the person in actual occupation and the rights remain undisclosed, the occupier would presumably be estopped from relying on such undisclosed rights. If the right should previously have been protected as a land charge and was not, then it will be void for non-registration and, therefore, there is nothing left which can be protected by actual occupation;
(c) a legal easement or profit (para.3). An equitable leasement cannot be overriding. This is because in unregistered land such a right must be protected as a D(iii) land charge. If it is, it will be translated into a notice on the register of title. If no land charge was entered, it will be void against a purchaser and cannot, therefore, be revived on first registration.

3. Rights which override registered dispositions. These are set out in Schedule 3 and include:

(a) legal leases of seven years or less (para.1);
(b) interests of persons in actual occupation (para.2). As above, this protection excludes strict settlements, spousal rights of occupation, overriding leases and certain reversionary tenancies. It also excludes:
  (i) the rights of a person of whom enquiry was made who failed to disclose the right when he reasonably should have done so (para.2(b));
  (ii) an interest which belongs to a person whose occupation would not have been obvious on a reasonably careful inspection of the land at the time of the disposition (para.2 (c)(i)) and of which the person to whom the disposition is made does not have actual knowledge at the time (para.2(c)(ii));
(c) a legal easement or profit which arises through by prescription or by implication (*e.g.* under the rule in *Wheeldon v Burrows* (1879) or by virtue of s.62 of the Law of Property Act 1925) and either:
  (i) (only if easement created after October 13, 2006) is within the actual knowledge of the purchaser; or
  (ii) (only if easement created after October 13, 2006) would have been obvious on a reasonably careful inspection of the land over which the easement or profit is exercisable; or,
  (iii) has been exercised within the period of one year before the disposition (para.3).

Rights which override: transitional provisions

These temporary provisions are designed to protect existing overriding interests and, thereby, preserve the established rights of third parties. These interim rights are detailed in Schedule 12 and, in brief, maintain:

(a) the overriding quality of leases which were previously overriding interests, *i.e.* a legal lease of less than 21 years (para.12);
(b) the rights of a person in actual occupation or *in receipt of rents and profits* from the land (para.8);
(c) existing legal easements and profits which were overriding interests prior to the 2002 Act (para.9).

Actual occupation and protection of rights

As shown, the rights of a person in actual occupation may amount to an unregistered interest which can override both first registration and a registered disposition. It is, therefore, important to understand the workings of this major incursion upon the mirror principle.

1. This overriding interest protects the rights of persons in actual occupation, not the occupation itself: *National Provincial Bank Ltd v Hastings Car Mart Ltd* (1964). Accordingly, it is necessary to show that there exists a property right that is capable of being protected and that the person claiming it is in actual occupation of the land. The right must subsist in reference to land (*i.e.* not merely be a personal right such as licence) and must not be excluded by the 2002 Act. For example, strict settlements, reversionary leases taking effect more than three months in the future and spousal rights of occupation are expressly excluded. Otherwise the rule is that any property right, whether legal or equitable, can be protected by occupation. This includes estoppel interests and mere equities (such as arise under *Barclays Bank v O'Brien* (1994) in relation to undue influence and misrepresentation). In *Williams & Glyn's Bank Ltd v Boland* (1981), it was held that a wife's beneficial interest under a trust of land could be protected by virtue of her occupation. This, of course, cannot occur if the interest has been overreached: *City of London Building Society v Flegg* (1988). In *Webb v Pollmount Ltd* (1966) an option to purchase the freehold was protected by the fact of occupation by the grantee as tenant.

2. Whether a person is in "actual occupation" is an issue of fact and the words must be given their ordinary and plain meaning. It does not matter that others may also occupy the land. Occupation of any part of the land in the title does not operate to secure protection of the whole. Only the rights relating to the part occupied will be protected. Occupation requires some element of physical presence, but a temporary or transient presence will not suffice. In *Strand Securities v Caswell* (1965), the presence of furniture without personal occupation was inadequate for these purposes. Preparatory steps before completion such as carrying out building work may also be insufficient: *Lloyds Bank plc v Rosset* (1991). In *Epps v Esso Petroleum Co.* (1973), regularly parking upon a strip of land was not regarded as being in actual occupation of the land. It is possible to occupy though an agent or member of the family (*e.g.* a caretaker employed to look after a flat), but a child in occupation of premises is not "in actual occupation" for its parent for the purpose of the section: *Hypo-Mortgage Services Ltd v Robinson* (1997). Temporary absences do not, however, prevent a person being in actual occupation. In *Chhokar v Chhokar* (1984), for example, a wife was in hospital having a baby and yet remained in occupation throughout. The duration of the absence and an intention to return appear to be the key factors.

3. As to the timing of actual occupation, occupation must exist when the transfer to the purchaser takes effect: *Abbey National Building Society v Cann* (1991). Moving into occupation subsequent to this time, but before registration of the of the purchaser's title, is not sufficient.

Alterations and indemnity

1. Registered title is a state guaranteed title, but even if a proprietor has absolute title there may be situations where, due to error or fraud, the register is inaccurate. For example, the reliability of title offered on first registration may later turn out to be unwarranted or an undisclosed interest affecting the land may subsequently emerge. Schedule 4 of the 2002 Act allows two forms of corrective response:

(a) "rectification" of the register in circumstances where there is the correction of a mistake which will "prejudicially affect" the title the registered proprietor (para.1). For example, where the wrong person has been registered as proprietor. Where the registered proprietor is in physical possession, the power to rectify is heavily curtailed. No order can be made without the registered proprietor's consent unless either he has by fraud or lack of care caused or substantially contributed to the mistake or it would be unjust for rectification not to occur;

(b) "alteration" of the register in circumstances where there is no resulting prejudice to the registered proprietor (para.2). An order may be obtained either from the court or the land registrar for alterations in order, first, to correct a mistake (*e.g.* where a land charge had not been protected by notice on first registration). Secondly, to bring the register up-to-date (*e.g.* when an entry was made as a result of fraud). Thirdly, to give effect to any right excepted from the effect of registration (*e.g.* when qualified title is registered and a defect in title is later established). The registrar (but not the court) has the extra power to alter the register to remove superfluous entries (para.5). As regards to alterations, there is no extra protection afforded to a registered proprietor who is in possession.

2. The payment of an indemnity from the public purse is available under schedule 8 for loss due to the rectification of the register (*e.g.* because of forgery or an error in marking of boundaries or mis-stating the length of a lease). This is the practical application of the "insurance principle" underpinning registered conveyancing. This indemnity is not generally available for mere alterations because, as they do not prejudicially affect the registered proprietor, technically there is no loss caused: *Re Chowood* (1933). Indemnity will be denied where the loss arises because of the fraud or lack of care of the claimant (para.5). If the claimant is only partly at fault, indemnity can be scaled down to reflect the degree of culpability (para.5(2)). A six year limitation period in which to claim indemnity applies (para.8).

Adverse possession

Sections 96–98 and schedule 6 to the LRA 2002 introduce a new regime for dealing with adverse possession (so called "squatter's rights"). A squatter will now be able to apply to be a registered proprietor with possessory title after 10 years adverse possession. The registered proprietor and others interested in the land will be notified of the application. If the application is unopposed within a period of two years, the squatter will become the new registered proprietor of the land. If it is opposed, the squatter will become the registered proprietor only if:

(a) it would be unconscionable because of an estoppel for the squatter to be dispossessed; or
(b) for some other reason, the squatter is entitled to be registered. For example, in *Bridges v Mee* (1957), the purchaser had paid the full purchase price, but the land was never conveyed to him. He moved into possession and later claimed title by adverse possession;

(c) where it is a boundary dispute and the squatter reasonably believed, for at least the 10 year period, that the disputed land was his.

6. LEASES

Introduction

1. A lease is an estate in land of defined duration. It is capable of being a legal estate under s.1(1)(b) of the Law of Property Act 1925 provided that it is a "term of years absolute" and is created in the correct manner (*i.e.* if exceeding three years by deed (ss.52, 54). A lease will usually carry with it an estate, but this is not necessarily the case: *Bruton v London & Quadrant Housing Trust* (2000) (see below).

2. The terms "lease", "term of years", "demise" and "tenancy" are interchangeable expressions. The landlord is often referred to as the "grantor" or "lessor" and the tenant as the "grantee" or "lessee". The landlord on granting a lease retains a "reversion" which is essential to the landlord and tenant relationship. Either the leasehold term or the landlord's reversion may be "assigned" (*i.e.* transferred) and the tenant may grant a "subtenancy" ("sublease" or "under-lease") for any period at least one day shorter than the period which he himself holds.

UNUSUAL LEASES

Perpetually renewable leases

1. A lease in perpetuity is void as it does not constitute a "term of years absolute". However, a perpetually renewable lease (*i.e.* one where the power of renewal is given as often as the lease expires) is saved by s.145 of the Law of Property Act 1922 and converted into a term of 2000 years.

2. Perpetually renewable leases are created accidentally by giving the tenant, as in *Caerphilly Concrete Products Ltd v Owen* (1972), the right to renew "on the same terms and conditions including this clause" or as in *Northchurch Estate v Daniels* (1947), by granting a renewal "on identical terms and conditions."

3. Only the tenant can terminate the converted 2000 year lease by serving 10 days' notice timed to expire on what would otherwise have been the renewal date.

Leases for life

1. Under s.149(6) of the LPA 1925, a lease at a rent or fine, for life or lives, or for any term of years determinable with life or lives or on the marriage of the lessee is automatically converted into a 90-year term. This includes:

    (a) a lease to X for life;
    (b) a lease to X for 10 years if he so long lives;
    (c) a lease to X for 99 years if he so long remains a bachelor.

2. Any lease within the section does not terminate on death or marriage (as the case may be) and instead continues after that time until either party gives at least one month's notice to the other (or heir). The notice must be timed to end on a quarter day.

THE INGREDIENTS OF A LEASE

For a lease to exist there must be:
1. *A capable grantor and grantee.* As made clear in *Rye v Rye* (1962), one cannot lease property to oneself. Where a landlord does not have the legal power to grant tenancies, the agreement cannot confer a leasehold estate: *Camden LBC v Shortlife Community Housing Ltd* (1992). Traditionally, only a licence could then be created, but, following *Bruton v London & Quadrant Housing Trust* (2000), it is now possible to have a purely contractual relationship which between (and only between) the parties may be categorised as a tenancy (see below).
2. *The commencement date of the lease must be certain.* If none is specified, it is assumed that the lease will commence on the tenant taking possession. By virtue of s.149 of the LPA 1925, the commencement date can only be delayed up to 21 years (in the meanwhile it is called a "reversionary tenancy").
3. *The duration of the lease must be certain* and capable of being ascertained at the beginning of the lease. This explains the policy why perpetual leases and leases for life have been converted by statute into definite periods of years;

4. *A rent* is usual and indicates a lease, but it is not necessary:
s.205(1)(xxvii) LPA 1925;
5. *Exclusive possession* (*i.e.* the legal right to exclude all others
from the property) must be granted.

Certainty of duration

With fixed term leases, there is no problem with certainty (*e.g.*
99 years is expressly defined). As the rule is concerned with
maximum duration, a forfeiture clause and a break clause do
not offend certainty. In relation to periodic tenancies (*e.g.*
monthly tenancies) they too satisfy the certainty requirement
and are somewhat artificially viewed as running from, say,
month to month until ended by notice to quit. If it is impossible
to calculate the duration of the term, then the lease is void: *Lace
v Chantler* (1944) (a lease for the duration of the war). A lease for
the "duration of Parliament" would, therefore, be invalid.
Similarly, a lease to continue "until the landlord requires the
land for road widening purposes" is invalid for uncertainty:
Prudential Assurance Co. Ltd v London Residuary Body (1992).
Other uncertain terms have included a lease to continue "so
long as the company is trading" (*Birrel v Carey* (1989)) and until
the repayment of a debt (*Canadian Imperial Bank v Bello* (1991)). If
a term is void for uncertainty, but the "tenant" has moved in
and paid rent then an implied, periodic tenancy may arise
instead (see below).

Exclusive possession

1. As mentioned, the right to exclusive possession is the right to
exclude all others from the premises, including the landlord. It
is the crucial test employed in distinguishing a lease from a
licence agreement. If there is no exclusive possession, there can
be no tenancy. The occupier will, instead, have mere permission
(whether contractual or not) to occupy. If exclusive possession is
granted, there will be (subject to limited exceptions: see below) a
tenancy.
2. Possession relates to legal rights and is not to be confused
with "exclusive occupation" which refers merely to physical
use.
3. The court's approach is to look at the substance and reality of
the transaction and to consider the agreement in the factual
matrix in which it exists: *Street v Mountford* (1985). Relevant

factors will include the relationship between the parties, the nature and extent of the property, the intended and actual use of the property and the real control retained by the landlord. Descriptive labels attached to the agreement are far from conclusive. The subjective intentions of the parties are largely irrelevant.

4. If the grantor remains in general control of the property (as with an inn, hotel or boarding house) a licence is likely to be inferred. In *Abbeyfield (Harpenden) Society v Woods* (1968), a resident in an old people's home was a licensee because of the services provided, and control retained, by the management.

5. If the contract attempts to exclude exclusive possession, the court will be watchful for shams, pretences and false terms: *Street v Mountford* (1985). If the attempt is not genuine and realistic, those parts of the agreement will be disregarded: *Antoniades v Villiers* (1990). The court will then give effect to what it considers to be the true bargain.

6. The *Street v Mountford* test extends beyond the residential market and applies also to commercial and agricultural property. Nevertheless, because of the widely different uses and structures of these types of property, it appears that exclusive possession can more easily be denied: *NCP v Trinity Development* (2001) (a licence of a car park).

7. In exceptional circumstances, even where exclusive possession exists, a licence rather than a tenancy may be inferred. These instances occur where there is a lack of intention to create legal relations between the parties, for example:

(a) *family arrangements*: in *Cobb v Lane* (1952), a brother was allowed to occupy premises and this was held to be a licence and not a tenancy. However, the existence of a family relationship does not automatically prevent a tenancy as can be seen from *Nunn v Dalyrymple* (1990) where a member of the landlord's family was allowed to occupy a cottage in return for regular rent payments and became a tenant. Each situation depends, therefore, upon the intention attributed to the parties and the inferences to be drawn from the circumstances of each case;

(b) *acts of friendship, charity and generosity*: in *Booker v Palmer* (1942) a licence was upheld when a homeless woman was allowed to occupy a cottage; see also *Gray v Taylor* (1998) which concerned occupancy of an almshouse;

(c) *employees*: a distinction has to be drawn between an employee who is genuinely required to occupy the premises for the better performance of his duties (*e.g.* a farm worker in a tied cottage) and an employee who occupies as a fringe benefit or an inducement to encourage the employee to work better: *Norris v Checksfield* (1991).

Multiple Occupancy Agreements

Where the premises are occupied by two or more persons, the occupiers will commonly share exclusive possession between themselves and become joint tenants under the lease. For a joint tenancy to exist, however, the so-called four unities (time, possession, title and interest) must be present. As in *AG Securities v Vaughan* (1990), it is possible to fragment the unities so as to prevent a joint tenancy arising. If the landlord rents out individual bedrooms in a house to four people previously unconnected with one another and they move in at different times, pay different amounts for the accommodation, hold under different types of contract with different terms then no legal alchemy can produce a joint tenancy. If the landlord reserves the right to replace departing occupiers and reallocate rooms, the occupiers are licensees because neither together nor individually can they be said to have exclusive possession. Even if each could be said to have a tenancy of a bedroom, none would enjoy security of tenure because, as they would share essential living rooms, none can be said to occupy a separate dwelling: *Uratemp Ventures v Collins* (2001).

GRANTING A LEGAL LEASE: FORMALITIES

1. A legal lease for any period greater than three years can only be created by deed: s.52(1) of the LPA 1925. No deed or writing is required at law for a lease which takes effect in possession; is for a term not exceeding three years (whether or not the lessee is given the power to extend the term); and is at the best rent reasonably obtainable without taking a fine: s.54(2). The term "possession" includes receipt of rent and profits from a sub-tenant: s.205. The definition by implication also incorporates periodic tenancies.
2. A deed is, however, required for any assignment of a legal lease and this includes one which has been created orally under the three-year exception: *Crago v Julian* (1992).
3. A deed is a formal document that expresses itself to be a deed and is signed, witnessed and delivered as a deed (s.1 of the Law of Property (Miscellaneous Provisions) Act 1989).

4. If the parties intended that there be granted a legal lease, but failed to comply with the necessary formalities (*i.e.* the need for a deed), the lease is equitable. Nevertheless, if either the agreement or the lease is in writing, it will be viewed as a valid contract to create a legal lease. As such, the court can award specific performance of that contract and order the parties to execute a deed. In the intervening period, it is said that "equity looks on that as done which ought to be done" which in *Walsh v Lonsdale* (1882) promoted the conclusion that "an agreement for a lease is as good as a legal lease". This is misleading, however, because an agreement for a lease is not as good as a legal lease for the following reasons:

(a) a contract is dependent upon the availability of specific performance which is a discretionary remedy and may not be granted if, for example, a tenant is in breach of his obligation: *Coatsworth v Johnson* (1886);

(b) a legal lease creates an estate enforceable *in rem* against all third parties, whereas an equitable lease or estate contract is not automatically binding upon a purchaser of the landlord's estate. In *unregistered* land, an equitable lease can be defeated by a bona fide purchaser for value of the legal estate without notice and, moreover, a land contract must be registered as a Civ land charge in order to bind a purchaser for money or money's worth. In *registered* land, an equitable lease and an estate contract are burdens that should be protected by entry on the charges register by virtue of a notice. Protection may also arise under the Land Registration Act 2002, if the equitable tenant is in actual occupation of the property.

Types of Tenancy

1. Periodic tenancy. Apart from by way of express agreement, a periodic tenancy may arise by implication in circumstances where a person goes into possession and pays rent. The precise period of the tenancy is geared according to how the rent is payable. For example, if rent is payable weekly then it is a weekly implied tenancy; if payable monthly it is a monthly tenancy. Such an implied tenancy is a legal term of years absolute and, by virtue of s.54(2) of the LPA 1925, does not need to be created by deed. In the absence of contrary agreement, a periodic tenancy can be determined by notice to quit given by either party which with a yearly tenancy is, usually, six calendar months; with a quarterly tenancy is one quarter's notice; with a monthly tenancy is one month's notice; and with a shorter residential tenancy at least four week's notice is required by the Protection from Eviction Act 1977.

2. Tenancy at will. This is the lowest estate known to the law because it is a tenancy of uncertain duration which is determinable at the will of the landlord, cannot be assigned and terminates upon the death of either party. Such a tenancy can arise expressly or by implication: *Javad v Aqil* (1991). It will usually be found where, with the consent of the landlord, the tenant has either moved into possession or is holding over at the end of a lease pending negotiation of a sale or new lease. A rent may be charged, but such payments are unlikely to convert a genuine tenancy at will into a periodic tenancy: *London Baggage v Railtrack* (2000).

3. Tenancy at sufferance. Where a tenant holds over after the expiry of a lease without the consent of the landlord, a tenancy at sufferance arises. This is only marginally better than being a trespasser. The tenant may be liable for double rent (yearly value of the land) and the landlord can claim possession at any time.

4. Tenancy by estoppel. For a tenancy by estoppel to arise there must be a representation by the landlord that a lease will be granted and the tenant must place detrimental reliance upon that representation. This reliance must, however, be reasonable. The notion is that it would be unconscionable for the landlord to renege on the representation made. The classic example is where the landlord has no title to grant a lease, but purports to do so. The estoppel will arise on the purported grant and, if the landlord subsequently acquires the relevant title, the lease will be perfected.

5. Tenancy without an estate. The House of Lords in *Bruton v London & Quadrant Housing Trust* (2000) recognised for the first time that it is possible to have a contractual relationship which acts between the parties as a lease, but without it conferring on the "tenant" any estate in land. In *Bruton*, a licence was granted to the occupier by a landlord who itself had no legal title to grant a tenancy because it also held under a licence. The traditional wisdom was that, as a landlord cannot give a better title than is possessed, Mr Bruton must necessarily be a licensee. His claim to enforce a statutory repairing right available only to tenants, therefore, appeared to be hopeless. Nevertheless, Lord Hoffmann recognised that, although a lease will normally carry with it an estate in land, it need not always do so. He concluded that the relationship of the parties could exist as a tenancy purely within the framework of the contract between them. Hence, he was able to enforce the repair obligations against his landlord. To the outside world, however, Mr Bruton remained a licensee. This contractual tenancy will not, therefore, attract security of tenure and cannot affect third parties. It is debatable whether the same decision would have been reached if it had, instead, been the landlord who sought to assert a tenancy against the occupier's wishes (*e.g.* so as to send bailiffs in to distrain a tenant's goods for rent).

How Leases End

Leases can end in a variety of ways, some by agreement and some as a result of unilateral action by one of the parties:

1. Expiry of time. In a lease for a fixed period, the contractual tenancy will automatically determine when that period expires. Beyond this time, the tenant may have security of tenure (essentially, the right to stay in ocupation) afforded by legislation such as the Rent Act 1977, the Housing Act 1988 and Part II of the Landlord and Tenant Act 1954.

2. Notice to quit. This is relevant only to periodic tenancies because a lease for a fixed period can only be determined prematurely if the lease so provides. For example, the lease may give either party a right to break a fixed term, say, at the end of the initial five years (this is known as a "break-clause"). If a joint tenancy exists, a notice to quit served by merely one of them will be valid: *Hammersmith & Fulham LBC v Monk* (1992). A notice to quit given by a tenant will automatically terminate any sub-tenancies which exist: *Pennell v Payne* (1995). The notice given must be clearly worded as, if it would mislead a reasonable landlord or tenant, it will be invalid: *Mannai Investment Co. Ltd v Eagle Star Assurance Co. Ltd* (1997).

3. Merger. This may occur when the freehold estate and leasehold estate become vested in the same person (*e.g.* if the tenant buys the landlord's reversion). The extinction of the lease is not automatic and is dependent upon merger being intended.

4. Surrender. It is possible for a tenant to give up the lease to the landlord, that is, to surrender the lease. This can arise expressly (which should be done by deed) or can occur by operation of law (*e.g.* landlord accepting the return of the tenant's keys: *Chamberlaine v Scally* (1992)). A tenant cannot, however, be forced to offer surrender and a landlord cannot be compelled to accept it. Following surrender, the tenant is released from liability on the covenants (except as to past breaches): *Deanplan v Mahmoud* (1992).

5. Enlargement. Under s.153 of the LPA 1925, a lease may be enlarged into a fee simple where the lease was originally for 300 years or more and there is still at least 200 years left unexpired. There must be no trust or right of redemption in favour of the reversioner and the lease must not be liable to forfeiture by re-entry for breach of covenant. There must be no monetary rent payable.

6. Disclaimer. This is a predominantly statutory right to repudiate the lease, *e.g.* a trustee in bankruptcy can disclaim an onerous lease under s.315 of the Insolvency Act 1986. Some rights to disclaim put an end to the lease whereas others (including s.315) merely put an end to future liabilities.

7. Forfeiture. The right to forfeit for breach of tenant's covenant (leasehold covenants are considered in Ch.13) is the most powerful of the landlord's remedies. It allows the landlord to re-enter and put a premature end to the lease. The right is, however, dependent upon the lease containing a forfeiture clause, *i.e.* a clause expressly giving the landlord a right to re-enter: *Clarke v Widmall* (1977). It is normal for fixed term leases to contain such a clause. The landlord may, however, waive a breach of covenant either expressly or by conduct and this will prevent forfeiture for that default. Conduct can amount to waiver when the landlord's acts are consistent only with the continued existence of the lease (*e.g.* if the landlord subsequently sues for or accepts rent: *Central Estates v Woolgar (No. 2)* (1972)). Understandably, the landlord must know of the breach before it can be waived: *Chrisdell v Johnson* (1987). Waiver on one occasion does not operate as a general waiver for continuing breaches in the future: s.148 of the LPA 1925.

Forfeiture Procedures

Unless the premises are an occupied dwelling, the landlord can physically and peaceably re-enter the land. This is not, however, a popular method of forfeiture. Instead, the landlord will institute a forfeiture action in either the county court or, exceptionally, the High Court. The procedure involved is both awkward and complex and the conditions that operate vary according to whether the breach is of a rental covenant or is, instead, of some other covenant:

1. Non-payment of rent.

(a) At common law, it is necessary for the landlord to make a formal demand for the exact sum due on the precise day it falls due. The need for a formal demand is frequently excluded in the lease. In any event, it is dispensed with when the rent is six months in arrears and there are insufficient goods on the premises to allow the arrears to be discharged through the remedy of distress: s.210 of the Common Law Procedure Act 1852.

(b) As a general principle, the law leans against forfeiture and will grant discretionary relief whenever possible: *Bank of Ireland Home Mortgages v South Lodge* (1997). Relief will be given if the arrears are paid off either before the hearing or within a later period specified by the court and it is just and equitable to do so. Sub-tenants and mortgagees have a similar right to relief and this is so even if the tenant does not apply for relief. If relief is granted, the landlord may be required to grant a term direct to the sub-tenant or mortgagee for a period not exceeding that which the tenant originally held. An application for relief for breach of rental covenant can be entertained within six months of the landlord's re-taking possession.

2. Breach of other covenants.
Different considerations apply where the breach is not rent related.

(a) Section 146 of the LPA 1925 provides that the landlord must serve on the tenant a notice which specifies the breach complained of; requires it to be remedied (if capable of being remedied) and requires compensation (unless the landlord waives this).

(b) After service of the s.146 notice, the landlord must allow a reasonable period of time (usually three months) for compliance before effecting a re-entry. As mentioned, it is usually advisable for the landlord to obtain a court order before re-taking possession.

(c) Some breaches are, however, incapable of being remedied, for example, a breach of a covenant against illegal or immoral use which attaches a stigma to the property (*Rugby School Governors v Tannahill* (1935): use of premises as a brothel) and a breach of covenant against assigning, sub-letting or parting with possession (*Scala House and District Property Co. v Forbes* (1974)). In such cases, the s.146 notice must specify the breach complained of and should, in order to cater for doubt, require remedy "so far as the same is capable of remedy". Any notice which does not comply with s.146 is void and forfeiture cannot lawfully take place.

(d) The tenant has a right to apply to the court for relief whilst the landlord is proceeding to enforce the forfeiture (*i.e.* at any time before the landlord has actually re-entered). Unlike with rental breaches, where the court has ordered forfeiture and the landlord has taken possession, relief ceases to be available. If the landlord has, instead, taken the self-help route of peaceable re-entry, a tenant may still apply for relief after a landlord has retaken possession: *Billson v Residential Apartments Ltd* (1992). In deciding whether to grant the tenant (or sub-tenant and mortgagee) relief, the court will take into account all the circumstances of the case.

3. Forfeiture for disrepair. If it is a covenant to repair that has been broken, additional formalities are imposed. These extra limitations apply to leases which were granted initially for longer than seven years and which still have at least three years remaining unexpired. The Leasehold Properties (Repairs) Act 1938 requires the tenant to be told in the s.146 notice of the right to serve a counternotice on the landlord. If a counternotice is served within twenty eight days of notification, the 1938 Act requires the landlord to obtain the approval of the court before forfeiture can occur. The court may allow the landlord to proceed if the value of the freehold has been substantially diminished, the breach needs to be remedied immediately and there are special circumstances that make it just and equitable to allow forfeiture to go ahead.

7. TRUSTS OF LAND

Introduction

Traditionally, *successive* interests in land could be created by way of a strict settlement under the Settled Land Act 1925 and *concurrent* interests could operate behind a trust for sale under the Law of Property Act 1925. The 1925 machinery has, however, been the subject of major overhaul by the Trusts of Land and Appointment of Trustees Act 1996. The major changes promoted by the Act are two-fold:

(i) it prevents the creation of any new strict settlements, but allows existing settlements to continue under the old rules. The trust for sale has, to all intents and purposes, been abolished and existing trusts for sale are converted into the newly styled "trusts of land";

(ii) new powers are created in favour of the trustees of land and the rights of beneficiaries are clarified.

The Strict Settlement

Given that existing settlements are to continue and remain to be governed by the old rules, it is still necessary to have some familiarity with the concept of a strict settlement and the rules that regulate it. The key features of settled land are:

1. A settlement is an arrangement which establishes a series of *successive* beneficial interests in favour of a number of persons. The strict settlement was primarily used to keep land in the family. An example would be where Blackacre is left by a father (A) to his wife (B) for life, remainder to his son (C) in fee simple. The person who creates the settlement A is known as the settlor; B is the tenant for life; and C is known as the remainderman. C will become absolutely entitled to the property when B dies.

2. Settled land is land held on statutory trust and, consequently, there are trustees who look after the interests of the benefici-

aries. The tenant for life has a dual role to play: first, the legal
estate will be vested in him as trustee for the beneficiaries of the
settlement. Others are likely also to be appointed under the SLA
as trustees of the settlement. Secondly, he will be a beneficiary
of the settlement entitled to an equitable life interest along with
those who are entitled in remainder. Only one of these classes of
beneficiaries is entitled to physical occupation at a given time.
This will be the life tenant, but once the life interest has ended
the remainderman will have the right to possession.

3. All settlements had to be made by two documents, namely a
trust instrument and a principal vesting deed: s.4(1) of the SLA
1925. The trust instrument (which was usually a private document) details the trusts (*i.e.* the beneficial interests of the
settlement), appoints the trustees and sets out any powers
(additional to those contained in the SLA) to be given to them.
Where a settlement was created by will, the will became the
trust instrument. The vesting deed or "assent" (which was a
public document) contained a description of the land to be
settled, named the trustees, listed additional powers given and
vested legal title in the tenant for life subject to the settlement
trusts. A purchaser would not have to bother with the details of
the settlement (this is called the "curtain principle"), but will
know that a trust exists and can, therefore, ensure that beneficial
interests are overreached (see below). If a vesting deed is not
executed in favour of a tenant for life, any purported dealings
with the land can take effect only as a contract to carry out the
transaction: s.13.

4. The general function of the SLA trustees is to act in a
supervisory role in order to safeguard the rights of those
interested under the trust. The specific functions of trustees are
varied and include:

(a) to act as the statutory owners where there is no tenant for
    life; or as "special statutory owners" on the death of a
    tenant for life;
(b) to give consent to certain transactions of the tenant for
    life; and to receive notice of when the tenant for life is
    exercising certain other transactions or powers;
(c) to receive and hold capital money;
(d) to execute vesting documents and documents of
    discharge;

(e) to exercise the powers of the tenant for life where he
    wishes to purchase the land; or where he has unreason-
    ably refused to exercise his statutory powers and a court
    order directs the trustees to act.

THE TENANT FOR LIFE

1. The tenant for life is the person under the settlement who has
all the statutory powers of management and control as well as
possessing the legal estate: s.177(1) of the SLA. He is the person
of full age who is for the time being beneficially entitled to
possession of the settled land for his life: s.19(1).
2. In certain cases, for example, where the person entitled is an
infant, there may be no tenant for life within the statutory
definition. The powers of the tenant for life are then exercised
by the "statutory owners" who are usually the trustees of the
settlement. If in any case there are two or more persons of full
age so entitled as joint tenants, they together constitute the
tenant for life: *Muir v Lloyds Bank Plc* (1992).
3. As to the powers of the tenant for life:

(a) the tenant for life can, in general, deal with his own
    limited interest as he pleases, but transactions will not
    necessarily bind his successors. As to the legal estate that
    is vested in him, there can be no disposition except as
    permitted by s.18. The tenant for life is trustee not only of
    the legal estate vested in him, but also of his powers;
(b) some of the powers stated below must not be exercised
    without notice being given to the trustees of the settle-
    ment: s.101(1). This applies to the tenant for life's powers
    to sell; exchange; lease; mortgage; or grant an option. In
    these cases, he must give one month's notice before the
    transaction or contract and this notice must be given to
    two or more trustees or a trust corporation. The trustees
    may waive notice and the notice required may need to be
    in general form only. A purchaser dealing bona fide with
    the tenant for life need not inquire whether notice has
    been given: s.101(5);
(c) the power to sell or exchange must be at the best
    consideration reasonably obtainable: s.39(1). A purchaser
    who is acting in good faith with the tenant for life is
    deemed to have given the best consideration reasonably
    obtainable: s.110. Where joint tenants constitute the tenant

for life and one wants to sell and the other does not, the court will not order sale in the absence of bad faith: *Re 90 Thornhill Road* (1970);

(d) to grant certain leases as permitted by s.41, for example, a residential lease up to a period of 50 years;
(e) to raise money on mortgage: s.71;
(f) to grant options. They must be in writing at the best price or rent and are not to be exercisable after ten years.

Consent of the trustees or the court

1. Such consents are required to effect certain improvements of the settled land and to defray the cost out of capital or for it to be raised by mortgage. If the improvements are not authorised they must be paid for out of income. The precise details of financing vary according to permanency of benefit as classified by Schedule 3 to the SLA 1925.

(a) Part I improvements are of lasting benefit such as drainage, irrigation and bridges. These can be financed out of capital and the tenant for life need not pay for them personally.
(b) Part II improvements are of a more doubtful lasting benefit, *e.g.* provision of housing for agents; repair of dry rot; boring for water. Here the trustees or the court have a discretion as to whether to request the setting up of a sinking fund requiring payment out of income.
(c) Part III improvements are of a transitory value, *e.g.* installation of electricity or the purchase of movable machinery. The trustees must require repayment from the tenant for life for such improvements.

Attempted limitation of the powers of the tenant for life

1. The Settled Land Act makes all powers (with minor exceptions) exercisable only by the tenant for life. It is the tenant for life who is in real control of the land and not the settlor or the trustees of the settlement. Although the settlement may supplement the powers given by the SLA, it cannot curtail them. Indeed, s.106 renders void any provision that attempts to prevent or discourage the tenant for life from exercising his statutory powers. For example, a requirement will be void if:

(a) it provided that the tenant for life will forfeit his interest in the land if he should exercise his power of sale or exchange; or,

(b) the consent of any third person is required before the tenant for life can exercise the statutory powers of sale or exchange.

2. Any provision is void only so far as it in fact "tends to prevent or discourage the exercise of the statutory powers". A problematic situation arises where a settlor provides a fund to be used for the maintenance and upkeep of the settled land while the tenant for life is in occupation. The prospect of losing such a fund may dissuade the tenant for life from exercising his powers of leasing or selling and, if so, the provision might be void.

Non-assignability of the powers of the tenant for life

A tenant for life is the trustee of the statutory powers and those powers cannot be relinquished: s.104. This general rule applies even if the tenant for life has parted with his own beneficial interest. Exceptions to this rule are when:

(a) the tenant for life has surrendered his interest to the person next entitled under the settlement;
(b) the tenant for life has ceased to have a substantial beneficial interest (whether by bankruptcy, assignment, incumbrance or otherwise) and has unreasonably refused to exercise the powers or consents to an order. The court may make an order authorising the trustees to exercise the statutory powers: *Re Thornhill Settlement* (1941);
(c) the tenant for life is a mental patient, the statutory powers being exercised by order of the Court of Protection.

Protection of a purchaser

In a general sense, the purchaser of settled land is protected by the machinery of overreaching. If a tenant for life exercises his statutory powers (such as selling or leasing the settled land) the interests of beneficiaries under the settlement should be over-reached (*i.e.* will not bind the purchaser). This is, however, dependent upon the purchase money being paid to at least two trustees or a trust corporation (see Ch.4). In dealing with any purchaser, the tenant for life must ensure that the best price reasonably obtainable is negotiated and that the provisions regarding vesting instruments and notice have been complied

with. The following statutory provisions protect the position of
the purchaser:

(a) a purchaser acting in good faith shall be deemed to have
given the best price obtainable and to have complied with
all the SLA provisions (s.110). This provision seemingly
applies whether or not the purchaser realises that he is
dealing with a tenant for life: *Re Morgan's Lease* (1972);
(b) a purchaser of a legal estate is not entitled to call for the
trust instrument (a private document), but may assume
that certain particulars stated in the vesting deed are true
(s.110(2));
(c) a person dealing in good faith with the tenant for life is
not concerned whether notice of an intended transaction
has been given to the trustees (s.101);
(d) the purchaser is not concerned as to how the proceeds of
sale paid to the trustees are distributed (s.95);
(e) any disposition by the tenant for life or statutory owners
which is not authorised by the Act is void except for the
purpose of binding the tenant for life's own beneficial
interest while it continues (s.18). A vesting deed will not,
however, be invalid because of any error in any of the
statements or particulars required to be within it (s.5(3)).

THE TRUST OF LAND

With the coming into force of the Trusts of Land and Appointment of Trustees Act 1996 the trust for sale mechanism has been
replaced by the trust of land. As the trust for sale has essentially
been consigned to the dustbin of legal history, it is unnecessary
to consider it here. Instead, it is crucial to understand the
provisions and workings of the 1996 Act.
1. The Act is based on the recommendations of the Law
Commission and came into force on January 1, 1997.
2. The Act defines a trust of land as "any trust of property
which consists of or includes land" The Act applies to all forms
of trust (whether express, implied or arising by operation of
law).
3. The creation of entailed interests is no longer possible,
although existing ones continue. Any attempt to create an
entailed interest after 1997 will create a fee simple, provided the
grantor has this interest.
4. The outmoded "doctrine of conversion" (whereby a beneficiary's interest was automatically deemed not to be in the land,

but rather in the proceeds of an eventual sale of the land) is abolished and beneficiaries under the trust of land hold an interest in land and not in money: s.3. One consequence of this is that undivided shares in land are now within the definition of land in s.205(1)(ix) of the LPA 1925.
5. Express and implied trusts share mainly the same characteristics: s.4.

Powers of trustees of land

1. Under the 1996 Act, legal title will be vested in the trustees and it is they who will have all the powers of an absolute owner for the purpose of exercising their functions as trustees.
2. In exercising their powers the trustees shall have regard to the rights of the beneficiaries. The trustees are under a duty to consult the beneficiaries and give effect to their wishes, in so far as is consistent with the purposes of the trust of land: ss.6 and 11 of the 1996 Act.
3. There is a new statutory power to purchase land and a revised one to partition (that is, physically to divide the property for so that each beneficiary can own a separate part): ss.6 and 7.
4. The powers of the trustees may be made subject to the consent of the beneficiaries, but only if this is provided for in the trust instrument or by order of the court.
5. The overreaching machinery applies fully to trusts of land.
6. Trustees of land may delegate to beneficiaries much the same powers as a tenant for life has under a strict settlement: s.9.
7. Under the 1996 Act whatever the instrument creating the trust of land provides, no more than two consents are needed by the trustees to exercise any function relating to the land in order for a purchaser to be protected. Although a minor's consent is not necessary to protect a purchaser, the consent of a parent or someone who has parental responsibility is required. The consent of a receiver of a mentally incapable person is required: s.10.
8. New rules on consultation with beneficiaries are provided in s.11. Trustees of land are required, so far as practicable, to consult the beneficiaries of full age and beneficially entitled to an interest in possession in the land when exercising any function relating to land subject to the trust. The trustees should, so far as is consistent with the general interest of the trust, give effect to the wishes of those beneficiaries or in case of dispute of

the majority: s.11. Where a new trust of land is created, the creators of the trust can "opt out" of the consultation obligation, and similarly existing trusts can be "opted in".

Sale of trust land

Trustees have wide powers of sale should they choose to exercise them. If the trustees cannot agree as to whether the land should be sold, they or any interested party, may apply to the court for it to make such order as it thinks fit: s.14 of the 1996 Act. If the trustees choose to exercise the power to sell, they have all the powers of an absolute owner. On a sale the proceeds are held for the beneficiaries whose interests in the land are likely to be overreached by the purchaser. Before exercising any power of sale, the trustees must obtain any consents required by the trust instrument and have consulted with the beneficiaries. After consultation the trustees should give effect to the wishes of the beneficiaries, provided that to do so would not be inconsistent with the purposes of the trust. If the trustees disagree between themselves, an order of the court may be necessary.

Rights of occupation

The 1996 Act attempts to state comprehensively the entitlement of beneficiaries to occupy the co-owned property. It confers a right of occupation and then specifies the circumstances in which it can be cancelled or modified. Section 12 allows a beneficiary who is not also a trustee to occupy the land at any time provided the land is available for occupation and occupation is not inconsistent with the trust of land. There is no s.12 right if the property is unavailable or unsuitable for occupation. A co-owner with legal title (*i.e.* a trustee) already has the right to occupy by virtue of having the legal estate. The right to occupy might be restricted under s.13 where there are two or more beneficiaries. The trustees might then exclude the entitlement of one or more beneficiaries (but not them all) to occupy. A co-owner already in occupation can be excluded only with his consent or by an order of the court. The trustees are required to act reasonably which means that they must, by virtue of s.13(4) consider the intentions of the person(s) who created the trust; the purpose for which the land is held; and the circumstances and wishes of each beneficiary who is otherwise entitled to occupy the property.

Attaching conditions

The trustees can attach conditions to a beneficiary's right to occupy: s.13(3). These conditions must be reasonable and can include a requirement that the occupier pay all outgoings and expenses in relation to the land. If a beneficiary is excluded from the land, the occupiers might be required by the trustee to pay a rent (by way of compensation for loss of the right) to an excluded co-owner: s.13(8).

Powers of the court

On the breakdown of a relationship, for example, one co-owner might want to sell the land and distribute the proceeds of sale between them. Another co-owner may not wish to sell and may seek to continue in residence. The 1996 Act caters generally for the court to resolve disputes as between co-owners themselves and as between co-owners and trustees (*e.g.* as to the exercise of the trustees' functions). As regards such disputes, s.15 provides a list of factors for the court to take into account. These are the intentions of the creators of the trust; the purposes for which the property subject to the trust is held; the welfare of any minor who occupies or might reasonably be expected to occupy the land and the interests of any secured creditor of any beneficiary. For example, if a couple separate then the purpose of the trust, which was to provide a family home for them both, has ceased. The court may well be persuaded to order sale in that situation. If, however, the couple have a young child then sale might be postponed until the child reaches school leaving age. To mini-mise hardship to the party who might be required to move out, the court could order a rent to be paid to the excluded co-owner: s.13(6). For example:

(i) in *Re Buchanan-Wollaston's Conveyance* (1939), there were four neighbouring property owners who combined to buy a piece of land that they desired to keep as an open space. The land was conveyed to them as joint tenants. The parties entered into a covenant in which they agreed to preserve the open space. One party wanted to sell up and applied to have the communal property sold. The court refused a sale as it would not allow a man in breach of his obligation to prevail;

(ii) in *Harris v Harris* (1996) the conclusive factor in determin-ing whether the land should be sold was the fact that the express trust deed stipulated that the property was to provide a home for father and son as long as either of them wished to stay there.

Insolvency

If the dispute as to sale is between the co-owners and a trustee in bankruptcy of one of them, very different considerations apply: s.15(4). The general rule is that the interests of the creditors should prevail and that sale should be ordered by the court: *Re Citro* (1991). This leaning in favour of the creditors is explicitly recognised in s.335A(2) of the Insolvency Act 1986. The bankruptcy court will deal with the matter and is obliged to make an order which is "just and reasonable" having regard to the interests of the creditor and the conduct and financial resources of the bankrupt's spouse (or former spouse), the needs of any children and all other circumstances. The needs of the bankrupt are, however, excluded from this consideration. If an application for sale is made more than one year after bankruptcy, the court must award sale unless the circumstances are exceptional. Sale might be refused, for example, where there is a resident child who is disabled or suffers from a serious long-term illness: *Re Bailey* (1977). In *Re Bremner* (1999), the bankrupt was dying of cancer and the court postponed sale until three months after his death.

Protection for purchasers

The overreaching provisions in s.2 of the LPA 1925 still apply so that if a purchaser pays capital money to at least two trustees or a trust corporation his interest prevails over any equitable interests arising under the trust. This applies both to unregistered and registered land: *City of London Builidng Society v Flegg* (1986). On termination of a trust, the trustees might be required to execute a deed of discharge. A purchaser will not need to check that trustees have obtained any consents required, consulted with beneficiaries or have acted in the best interests of any beneficiaries.

Single trustee protection

Where land subject to co-ownership is sold, as shown the purchaser should normally transfer the purchase money to at least two trustees. However, where there is a sole survivor in law and equity a purchaser of *unregistered* land is protected and will obtain good title if he pays the proceeds of sale to the single trustee. This is because of the Law of Property (Joint Tenants) Act 1964, as amended, which provides that a purchaser from a surviving *joint tenant* will get a good title, free from any trust interest created, if the surviving joint tenant conveys as beneficial owner. A purchaser will not, in those circumstances, need to appoint a second trustee so as to effect overreaching. The protection of the 1964 Act does not extend to registered land because the existence of another's beneficial interest should be revealed by the entry of a restriction on the Land Registry. If no restriction is entered, the purchaser will normally get a good title.

8. CO-OWNERSHIP

This chapter deals with concurrent co-ownership of land, that is, where two or more persons are entitled to simultaneous enjoyment of land. For example, the grant of Blackacre "to X and Y in fee simple" or "to X and Y in equal shares" creates co-ownership. As shown in the Ch.7, this is in contrast to where land is granted consecutively as "to X for life; then to Y in fee simple" which creates a strict settlement and no co-ownership exists. The law relating to co-ownership can be found in the common law rules, the structures of the 1925 property legislation and the provisions of the Trusts of Land and Appointment of Trustees Act 1996. There are two types of co-ownership in land that have any modern significance: the joint tenancy and the tenancy in common.

The Joint Tenancy

In the eyes of the law, joint tenants do not have separate shares in the land nor, indeed, any individual existence. They are regarded together as making up a single legal entity, *i.e.* a single owner. Individually, they own nothing, but they do have rights exercisable against each other (*e.g.* a monetary claim on any eventual sale). The joint tenancy is favoured by the common law. The outstanding feature of the joint tenancy is the right of survivorship (*ius accrescendi*).

1. Survivorship. On the death of one joint tenant, his interest in land passes to the survivors automatically by right of survivorship. This process continues until eventually only one owner survives. At that point, co-ownership ceases and the sole survivor becomes absolutely entitled to the land. There is no conveyance and no death duties to be paid. The right of survivorship is not ousted by a joint tenant's will. This right might be advisable in relation to the family home, but is clearly unsuited to an investment venture between partners or friends.

2. The four unities. A joint tenancy cannot exist unless the four unities exist: *AG Securities v Vaughan* (1990). The unities are:

(a) *unity of possession.* Each co-owner must be entitled to possession of any part of the land and entitled to possession of the whole land with the others. This does not mean that the co-owners must all actually occupy the property. If one occupier moves out a joint tenancy will continue unaffected. It is to do with legal entitlements (which Parliament can modify, *e.g.* under domestic violence legislation or under the Trusts of Land and Appointment of Trustees Act 1996) and not de facto use;

(b) *unity of interest.* The interest of each joint tenant must be identical in extent, nature and duration. One cannot have a larger interest than another. No joint tenancy is, therefore, possible between a freeholder and a leaseholder. Similarly no single joint tenant can sell or lease the land because he does not have the whole legal estate. An attempt to do might amount to a severing event: see below. All the joint tenants must assent and join in the transaction. Similarly, the surrender of a lease must be made by all joint tenants as must the exercise of a break clause in a lease. Paradoxically, a notice to quit under a periodic tenancy given by one of several joint tenants will be valid: *Hammersmith and Fulham L.B.C. v Monk* (1992). As each new period amounts to a renewal of the tenancy, the unwillingness of one joint tenant is fatal to the continuance of the tenancy;

(c) *unity of title.* All joint tenants must claim title under the same act or document, for example, by the same conveyance or by the same act of adverse possession;

(d) *unity of time.* The joint tenants' interests must all vest (*i.e.* have been acquired) at the same time.

Consequences of a joint tenancy

A joint tenancy has the following features:
1. Each co-owner has a "potential' share in the property. If there are four co-owners, each has a potential one-quarter share of the proceeds of sale. They are entitled to any rents and profits pending sale in the same proportions.
2. The joint tenancy will continue until only one survivor is entitled to the land by way of survivorship.
3. Any joint tenant can convert his joint tenancy into a tenancy in common by way of severance (see below).

The Tenancy in Common

This form of co-ownership is favoured by equity and differs from a joint tenancy in the following ways:
1. Tenants in common hold in individual shares, *i.e.* they have distinct, notional shares in the land that has not yet been divided between the co-owners. Although each tenant in common has a separate interest, it is not possible to say who owns what piece of the land.
2. There is no right of survivorship. The size of the tenant in common's share is fixed and is unaffected by the death of any other tenant in common. The tenant in common can leave his share by will and, if not, it will pass on intestacy to his next of kin.
3. Of the four unities only unity of possession is essential. Without this there can be no co-ownership at all. There would, instead, be individual ownership of distinct parts.
4. The size of the shares of each tenant in common need not be equal. For example, one tenant in common may have a 60 per cent share whereas the other may have a 40 per cent stake.
5. If all the tenants in common agree, they can execute a deed conveying the land to them as joint tenants. This formal act would convert their tenancy in common into a joint tenancy.

The Co-ownership Trust

All forms of co-ownership must exist behind a trust of land: ss.4–5 of the 1996 Act. This means that there is a fragmentation of legal and equitable ownership.

As regards legal title:

(a) the legal estate must be held by one or more trustees. If there is more than one trustee, the legal title must always be held as joint tenants. There can be no tenancy in common of the legal estate: s.1(6) of the LPA 1925. It is impossible, therefore, to convert a joint tenancy at law into a tenancy in common at law;

(b) there can only be a maximum of four trustees who hold the legal estate. The trustees will be named in the conveyance and, if more than four are named, the legal estate is vested in the first four named in the conveyance who are of full age and capacity and who are willing to act: s.34(2) of the Trustee Act 1925. Consequently the number of trustees cannot be increased beyond four. The following examples serve to illustrate:

  (i) a conveyance to A and B who are of full age and capacity. A and B hold the legal estate as trustees on a statutory trust of land as joint tenants at law for the benefits of themselves as co-owners in equity;

 (ii) a similar conveyance to A, B, C, D and E. Here the first four hold the legal estate as trustees for the benefit of all five in equity;

(iii) a conveyance to X and Y to hold for the benefit of A, B and C. Here the trustees have been expressly named and X and Y hold the legal estate on trust of land for the benefit of A, B and C as co-owners in equity.

The beneficial interests

The trustee(s) hold the legal estate for the persons entitled in equity on the terms of the trusts that may be express, implied or imposed by statute. The equitable (or beneficial) interests may take effect behind the trust either as joint tenants or tenants in common. It is here, therefore, that true entitlement lies and the distinction between a joint tenancy and a tenancy in common assumes major importance. Working out which type of co-ownership has been created will turn upon such matters as the presence of the four unities (all are necessary for a joint tenancy); the stated purpose of the conveyance (*e.g.* it may expressly declare that the beneficial entitlement is to be as joint tenants); words used in the conveyance (there might be words used which are consistent only with a tenancy in common); and any presumptions which the court may invoke (the common law favours a joint tenancy whereas equity favours a tenancy in common).

Joint tenancy or tenancy in common?

As indicated a four-stage approach should be adopted in order to determine which type of co-ownership is to regulate the beneficial interests under the trust.

(a) Are the four unities present? If so, then it can be a joint tenancy; if not, it most certainly cannot be a joint tenancy. This means that the four unities are a necessary, but not decisive, condition for the existence of a joint tenancy;

(b) If the unities are present, is there an express declaration in the conveyance? If the parties declare themselves to be joint tenants or to be tenants in common, this will usually be decisive: *Roy v Roy* (1996). For example "to A, B, C and D as joint tenants at law and in equity" will normally be conclusive of a joint tenancy. If the conveyance declares the existence of a tenancy in common, this will always be decisive;

(c) If the unities are present and there is no declaration of a tenancy in common, are any "words of severance" used in the grant? Words of severance are terms and expressions that clearly indicate a tenancy in common. Examples would include, "share", "equally", "amongst" and "divided between". In *Martin v Martin* (1989) a tenancy in common emerged as the words "in equal shares" were used. These words indicate that the co-owners have separate interests in the land;

(d) If the above tests do not operate, are there any evidential presumptions which can help the court? The common law presumes that a joint tenancy has been created and this presumption will prevail except where equity will intervene. This limited intervention will arise where:

  (i) the purchase money is provided in unequal shares, a tenancy in common in proportion to the share of the money advanced is presumed: *Bull v Bull* (1955). In *Malayan Credit Limited v Jack Chia* (1986), rent payable in unequal shares was equivalent to providing the purchase money in unequal shares and, therefore, a tenancy in common was presumed;

  (ii) the money is advanced on mortgage, whether in equal or unequal shares a tenancy in common is presumed between the lenders. Each means to lend his own and take back his own: *Vickers v Cowell* (1839);

(iii) the land is acquired by business partners as part of partnership assets a tenancy in common is presumed: *Lake v Craddock* (1732). No formal partnership is required and the rule applies to any joint undertaking with a view to profit. The right of survivorship has no place in business.

Severance of the joint tenancy

It is to be emphasised that the *legal estate* must always be held on a joint tenancy and cannot be severed, *i.e.* converted into a tenancy in common. Severance is only possible in respect of the *beneficial interests* of the co-owners. As demonstrated in *Williams v Hensman* (1861), a joint tenancy behind a trust can be converted into a tenancy in common in a number of ways:

(a) *Acting on one's share.* The clearest method of severance is to alienate (sell or otherwise dispose of) one's own interest to a stranger or, indeed, another joint tenant. This must occur *inter vivos* (*i.e.* be a lifetime dealing) and cannot, therefore, be effected by will. The act must be final and binding which means that there must generally be a valid contract to deal with the land. A mere statement of intention is insufficient. Where a joint tenant sells his potential share, the purchaser becomes a tenant in common as to that share and other joint tenants (provided there are more than one) remain joint tenants as to the rest of the estate. The alienation may be involuntary, for example, where the interest in the joint tenancy passes to a trustee in bankruptcy on insolvency: *Re Dennis* (1996). Partial alienation by mortgaging one's share or creating a lease or life interest also severs the joint tenancy. Similarly, the commencement of litigation may amount to an act on one's share provided that the court action directly concerns the joint tenancy itself. Commencing divorce proceedings, for example, would not sever a joint tenancy between estranged husband and wife.

(b) *Mutual agreement of the joint tenants.* The joint tenants can act together and effectively agree to sever their joint tenancy. This is more informal than acting on one's share and does not need a valid contract. It must, however, be such that it shows a common intention to sever. The parties must have reached a definite understanding and a fixed mutual attitude to sever: *Slater v Slater* (1987). For example, if the joint tenants agree that, on death, their shares will pass to their next of kin this will be a severing event: *McDonald v Morley* (1940). Similarly, if the joint tenants agree that, on sale, the proceeds should be divided (whether equally or unequally) a tenancy in common will immediately arise.

(c) *Mutual conduct of existing joint tenants.* This covers any course of dealing which intimates that the interests of all were mutually regarded as having been severed. The conduct must fall short of an express or implied agreement, but must show an unambiguous, common intention to sever. For example, where the co-owners execute mutual wills. It is not the wills themselves which sever, but rather the intention which underlies them shows the decision to sever: *Re Wilford's Estate* (1879). Similarly, inconclusive negotiations in relation to disposing of the co-owners' respective shares could sever the joint tenancy.

(d) *Homicide.* A person cannot benefit from his crime so that if one joint tenant unlawfully kills another he cannot take any benefit by way of survivorship: *Cleaver v Mutual Reserve Fund* (1892). The Forfeiture Act 1982, however, gives the court a limited discretion to override this rule (but not with murder) where it is just to do so. It appears that the consequences of the forfeiture rule will vary according to how many other joint tenants remain alive:

  (i) A and B hold as joint tenants at law and in equity. A murders B. A then holds the legal estate for himself and the estate of B as tenants in common in equity: *Schobelt v Barber* (1967);

  (ii) A, B and C hold as joint tenants at law and in equity. A murders B. A and C hold the legal estate as joint tenants on trust for B's estate and themselves as tenants in common. If A and C were allowed to remain as joint tenants, it would mean that A achieved some potential benefit from his crime (*i.e.* the tontine effect: there would be one less joint tenant to take under the right of survivorship);

  (iii) A, B, C and D hold as joint tenants at law and in equity and A murders B. A, C and D hold the legal estate as joint tenants on trust for A and B's estate as tenants in common and for C and D as joint tenants. Neither C nor D has committed any wrongdoing and neither profit from their own actions. It would be unfair on C and D, as well as being illogical, if their joint tenancy was severed by the criminal activity of A.

(e) *Notice in writing* under s.36(2) LPA 1925. If a joint tenant desires to sever the joint tenancy unilaterally he can achieve this by giving *all* the other joint tenants clear notice in writing of this desire. The notice must show an immediate intention to sever and not merely be a statement of future aspiration: *Harris v Goddard* (1983). A notice which has been posted, but not received remains effective for these purposes: *Re 88 Berkeley Road* (1971). In *Kinch v Bullard* (1998), a wife posted a letter notifying severance to her husband in respect of the matrimonial home. The husband was dying in hospital at the time and did not receive the notice. The wife thought she would now prosper better with the right of survivorship and destroyed the notice. The court held that there was severance despite the fact that the husband never actually received the notice. In *Re Drapers Conveyance* (1969), the issue of a summons by a wife claiming a sale of the matrimonial home amounted to notice for this purpose. In *Harris v Goddard* (1983), however, no severance occurred where a divorce petition had been served on a husband which merely stated that an order might be made at a future time in respect of the matrimonial home.

TERMINATION OF CO-OWNERSHIP

Co-ownership can end in a variety of ways:

(a) *Partition*: this is a mechanism whereby the land is physically divided between the co-owners. The joint tenants must be of full age and partition must normally be effected by deed. On partition each co-owner becomes absolutely entitled to a separate plot of land. Under s.7 of the Trusts of Land and Appointment of Trustees Act 1996 Act the trustees of land have powers of partition.

(b) *Overreaching*: where the trustees transfer title to a purchaser, and the purchase money is paid to at least two trustees or a trust corporation, the beneficiaries' interests are overreached and the co-ownership terminates.

(c) *Union in sole ownership* (merger): this will occur where all the legal and beneficial interests are finally vested in one person. For example, when only one joint tenant remains alive; when there is release by one joint tenant of his interest to the other; and where tenants in common leave their interest by will or intestacy to a remaining co-owner.

Family Home Rights

1. A spousal right of occupation in the matrimonial home is given by the Family Law Act 1996. This arises where a spouse does not own the legal estate of the matrimonial home. An interest under a trust does not deprive the spouse of this statutory protection. The right does not extend to property purchased after separation and lasts only until divorce. The rights are gender neutral in that they can be relied upon by either husband or wife. The right is registrable as a Class F land charge under the LCA 1972 or, in the case registered land, can be protected by a notice under the LRA 2002. Such rights cannot constitute overriding interests in respect of registered land.

2. If one spouse makes a substantial contribution in money or money's worth to the improvement of the matrimonial home a beneficial share will arise and the courts will quantify this share according to what seems just in all the circumstances: s.37 of the Matrimonial Proceedings and Property Act 1970. This is in addition to any trust interest that the spouse may already have. A similar rule extends to those who are engaged to be married: s.2(1) of the Law Reform (Miscellaneous Provisions) Act 1970.

3. Under the Matrimonial Causes Act 1973, on the breakdown of a marriage the court has wide discretionary powers to order a distribution of the spouses' property (this is called a "property adjustment order").

4. The Family Law Act 1996 makes provision not only for spouses, but also for cohabitants who have lived together as husband and wife or who intend to so occupy a home by providing a personal "matrimonial home right" of occupation. This extends also to same sex relationships. The cohabitant can apply for a court order protecting his or her occupation of the family home. If made, the order is only temporary and cannot bind a purchaser of the property.

CO-OWNERSHIP AND IMPLIED TRUSTS

1. The general rule is that the ownership of the legal estate carries with it the beneficial interest. This presumption can, however, be displaced by the statements and acts of the parties.

For example, if land is held in the name of one person, but the purchase price was provided by more than one person this may give rise to the courts implying a resulting trust or a constructive trust. Traditionally, there was a clear distinction between these types of trust. A resulting trust resulted from payments towards the purchase of the property: *Dyer v Dyer* (1788). Constructive trusts arose from agreements and understandings that the property would be shared on the strength of which the other acted to his or her detriment: *Grant v Edwards* (1986). In recent times, this distinction has become somewhat blurred. Following the decision of the House of Lords in *Lloyds Bank v Rosset* (1990), it appears that whenever a trust of the family home is implied it will be a constructive trust. There is, however, controversy and differing views as to the present state of the law. Even the Law Commission admitted in 1995 that, "The present legal rules are uncertain and difficult to apply and can lead to serious injustice".

2. There are two rules that emerge from the *Rosset* case:

  (a) **Rule 1** is where there is evidence that the parties discussed ownership and as a result reached an understanding, arrangement or agreement to share the property beneficially. If the other has acted detrimentally on this assurance (*i.e.* significantly altered his or her position), then that party will have a beneficial interest arising either by a constructive trust or an estoppel. It appears that the same outcome will be reached whether the court proceeds by imposing a constructive trust or by enforcing an estoppel. The courts, however, seem to favour a trust analysis: *Clough v Killey* (1996). This is the classic territory for the express bargain constructive trust and the resulting trust has never operated in such circumstances. The intention to share, however, needs to be express and communicated: *Springette v Defoe* (1992). This rule is arbitrary in that it depends upon a discussion having taken place. For example, in *Eves v Eves* (1975) a woman was told that the property was vested solely in the man's name simply because she was under 21 years of age. She was led to believe that the property belonged to them both jointly and a constructive trust arose. If no discussion occurs, then the rule simply does not apply: *Burns v Burns* (1984). Where there is an agreement as to the proportions each is to have, that understanding will be enforced:

Clough v Killey (1996). For example, if A says to B "come live with me and the house is half yours" that should give rise to a trust which gives B a 50 per cent interest. If the share is unspecified, the court will calculate what is fair and just in all the circumstances, including time and effort spent running the home and the family: *Drake v Whipp* (1996). The consideration is, most certainly, not limited merely to financial contributions.

(b) **Rule 2** applies where there is an absence of express discussion. In this situation, the court looks in detail at the conduct of the parties with the prospect of presuming a common intention to share beneficial ownership. If the common intention is discerned, it will give rise to an implied bargain constructive trust. This is, however, territory previously occupied by the resulting trust. For a constructive trust to arise, the claimant must have made some direct financial contribution to the (initial or on-going) purchase of the property. If the contributions are purely indirect (*e.g.* looking after the kids, paying household expenses, financing improvements (unless married or engaged: see above), decorating and house cleaning, there will be no grounds to justify the inference of a common intention to share: *Burns v Burns* (1984). Once the trust is activated by direct contributions, however, the court can take into account other circumstances in quantifying the claimant's share.

3. Resulting or constructive trust?

It is curious that, in *Lloyds Bank v Rosset* (1990), Lord Bridge avoided any reference to the implied resulting trust. Instead, he spoke consistently of an implied constructive trust operating under both rules. Some commentators believe that, as regards the second rule, this was a mistake of terminology (*i.e.* that Lord Bridge had really meant to say "resulting trust" and not "constructive trust"). This is unconvincing and has not been supported by any of the numerous cases that have followed in the wake of *Rosset*. The selection of the constructive trust must, therefore, have been deliberate. To understand this choice, it is necessary to appreciate that a resulting trust is founded upon arithmetical principles *i.e.* you get out in proportion to what you put in: *Re Densham* (1975). Hence, if there is 20 per cent contribution to the purchase price under a resulting trust the contributor will get back 20 per cent of the selling price—no more and no less. The share is fixed at the time of purchase. This is fine with arms' length transactions, but can be unjust in relation to cohabitants. Under a constructive trust, however, the court will calculate the share according to what is fair and reasonable having regard to all the circumstances, including any contribution to the purchase price. For example, in *Drake v Whipp* (1996), the claimant would under a resulting trust have had a 19.4 per cent share (£43,650). The court, however, calculated her share under constructive trust principles and gave her a share quantified at £75,000. Clearly, the constructive trust is more flexible and offers a fairer redistribution of family assets than that afforded by the cold mathematics underlying the resulting trust. This perhaps explains why Lord Bridge preferred the use of the constructive trust.

As to the role of the resulting trust, this will now it seems be largely confined to non-cohabitation cases. For example, X provides the money for a deposit on a house that P is to purchase and to live in alone. Unless regarded as a mere gift or loan, this would give rise to a purchase money resulting trust. The entitlement of X as a tenant in common would be fixed at this stage. This would be the inferred intention of both P and X at the date of the purchase. Traditionally, the resulting trust is ill-equipped to respond to any future contributions made by X. Accordingly, if X subsequently moves in with P and makes further direct or indirect contributions, a constructive trust should then arise to reflect those changing circumstances and intentions. The nature of the bargain has now changed and this must be reflected in the shift towards a constructive trust.

The purchaser of co-owned land

1. In *unregistered land*, the equitable interest created under a trust of land is not registrable by way of a land charge and is subject to the overreaching machinery, provided the conveyance is made by at least two trustees. As shown, in the case of single owners, overreaching does not apply and the situation is, instead, governed by the ancient doctrine of notice. There has been some dispute as to whether a purchaser of unregistered land has constructive notice of the rights of an occupying spouse. In *Caunce v Caunce* (1969), the presence of a wife in the matrimonial home was deemed not to constitute notice to the purchaser. The purchaser was not expected to act as a

"snooper" and "busybody". This rule was criticised in *Williams & Glyn's Bank Ltd v Boland* (1981) and *Kingsnorth v Tizard* (1986) and the modern view is that, as a wife's presence is separate from that of her husband, her occupation in the property is deemed to give constructive notice to the purchaser. This is so only when her presence should have been detected on a reasonably careful inspection of the property.

2. In *registered land*, in the absence of overreaching the interest of a co-owner in occupation of the family home can bind a purchaser. In *Williams & Glyn's Bank Ltd v Boland* (1981), a husband held the matrimonial home on trust for sale for himself and his wife. He mortgaged the house to the Bank and defaulted on the repayments. The Bank sought to take possession prior to selling the property. Mrs Boland argued that she had a beneficial interest which, because of her occupation, was binding on the Bank. The House of Lords held that her interest did, indeed, bind the Bank. This is because the rights of a person in actual occupation will usually constitute what is traditionally called an overriding interest, *i.e.* these rights do not need to be otherwise protected in order to bind a purchaser. The law is now as set out in the Land Registration Act 2002 (see Ch.5). A trust interest cannot be noted on the register by entry of a notice. It can, however, be protected by the entry of a restriction, but as shown this is usually unnecessary if the beneficiary is in actual occupation.

Beneficiaries and mortgage lenders

Much litigation has concerned an occupier with a beneficial interest attempting to enforce that interest against a mortgagee. A major distinction has emerged from these cases:

1. When the mortgage is entered in order to finance the initial purchase of the family home (*i.e.* an acquisition mortgage), the lender is in the strongest position. First, the occupier will not usually be in occupation at the key time when the mortgage is created: *Abbey National Building Society v Cann* (1991). Secondly, the beneficial co-owner will or should know that the purchase is mortgage assisted and is, therefore, deemed to have consented to his rights being relegated behind those of a mortgagee: *Paddington Building Society v Mendelsohn* (1985); *Bristol & West Building Society v Henning* (1985). Once consent to the original mortgage is given or implied, that consent will extend to a later re-mortgage, but only up to the same amount: *Equity & Law Home Loans Ltd v Prestridge* (1992).

2. When the mortgage is not contemporaneous with the purchase (*i.e.* it is what is called "a second mortgage" or non-acquisition mortgage), the lender is more vulnerable. The beneficial co-owner will now, in all likelihood, be in occupation. Subject to overreaching, the lender in the capacity of purchaser will, therefore, have constructive notice of the trust interest (unregistered land) or take subject to it as an interest that overrides registration (registered land). The lender will try to protect itself against such claims by obtaining from all occupiers an express disclaimer of their rights. This disclaimer of rights will be overturned only if it was induced by the misrepresentation and/or undue influence of the borrower: *Barclays Bank v O'Brien* (1994) (see Ch.10).

9. EASEMENTS

Introduction

An easement is an incorporeal right annexed to land either to use (a positive easement) or, less usually, to restrict the use of (a negative easement), the land of another. The term derives from the Old French term "aisement" and means something that makes the enjoyment of land easier. The types of easements that can exist are varied and include rights to use a neighbour's lavatory, to use a neighbour's washing line, to mix manure on a neighbour's land, to affix an advertising hoarding to a neighbour's building and to nail trees to an neighbour's wall. The major examples, however, are a right of way, a right of support and a right to light. An easement must confer a benefit on land (the dominant tenement) and burden other land (the servient tenement). It is often said that the categories of easement are never closed and that new rights might be admitted into the class as appropriate. An easement must be distinguished from:

(a) a *profit à prendre* which is a right to enter another's land and take something from the land which is naturally there (*e.g.* crops, timber, fish and animals). There is no need for a dominant tenement here as a profit can exist in gross. An easement offers no right to remove something from the land;

(b) a *licence* which is mere permission to do something on the servient land. This might be gratuitous (*i.e.* without consideration) or contractual. It is never an interest in land, there is no need for a dominant tenement and it cannot bind third parties. The rights that can be the subject of a licence are, however, much wider than those captured by the law of easements;

(c) a *restrictive covenant* which is an agreement to restrict the use of land for the benefit of other land. Freehold covenants are equitable interests only, cannot be acquired by long user and cover a wider range of restrictions than those subject to the few negative easements that can exist;

(d) *natural rights* which, unlike easements, emerge automatically from nature and do not depend upon another's grant. For example, a right to water flowing naturally through a defined channel;

(e) *public rights* which are exercisable by the general public (*e.g.* a public right of way). There is no need for any dominant tenement and the rights are never the subject of a grant;

(f) *a right under the Access to Neighbouring Land Act 1992* which makes provision to enable a person to gain access to neighbouring land in order to carry out works which are reasonably necessary for the preservation of his own land. This allows the court to grant an "access order" for the purpose of effecting repairs. This is not an easement, but is more than a mere licence. It is a statutory right effected by court order. The order can be made subject to such terms and conditions as the court deems necessary to avoid loss, damage and inconvenience to the landowner. In unregistered land, an access order can be registered in the register of writs and orders affecting land. In registered land, the Land Registration Act 2002 allows it to be protected by entry of a notice.

Status of an Easement

An easement is one of the four interests listed in s.1(2) of the Law of Property Act 1925 as having the capacity to exist as a legal interest. Whether it is legal or not depends upon its duration (a legal easement must be timed to reflect either a freehold or leasehold) and the manner of its creation. If it is created by deed, it will be legal: s.52. If it fails to satisfy either of these conditions, it will necessarily be an equitable easement. The *benefit* of an *existing* easement (whether legal or equitable) will automatically pass to a purchaser of the dominant land by virtue of s.62 of the LPA. This is primarily a word saving provision which entails that the seller does not have to assign the benefit expressly on each conveyance. As to whether the *burden* of an existing easement will pass on the sale of the servient land, this issue will turn upon whether the easement is legal or equitable and whether the land is unregistered or registered (see below).

Ingredients of an Easement

It was laid down in *Re Ellenborough Park* (1956) that there are four essential characteristics of an easement.

1. There must be both a dominant tenement and a servient tenement which means, essentially, that there must be one piece of land which carries the benefit and another which carries the burden. An easement cannot, therefore, exist "in gross" independent of ownership in land. In *London & Blenhein Estates v Ladbroke Retail* Parks (1993) there was no easement because the potential servient tenement had been transferred *before* the dominant tenement had been acquired. A right given to a person with no dominant land will usually fall to be classified as a licence.

2. The right must "accommodate" (*i.e.* benefit) the dominant tenement or a business carried out there. This means that the right "must have some natural connection with the estate as being for its benefit" (*per* Byles J. in *Bailey v Stephens* (1862)). The test, simply put, is whether the right makes the dominant tenement a better and more convenient property. A right to free tickets at a neighbouring football ground might increase the value of the dominant land, but it has nothing to do with the use of the land and cannot be an easement. In contrast, a right that improves the general utility of the dominant tenement, say, by giving a means of access or light clearly accommodates the land.

   (a) As to trade, in *Moody v Steggles* (1879) it was held that the right to fix an advertising sign to an adjoining property accommodated the business of a public house operating on the dominant land. It has to advertise the business, however, and not merely some product sold there. Hence, a sign adjacent to a supermarket that simply states "Drink Milk" is unlikely to bestow a sufficiently direct benefit on the business conducted on the dominant land. It should, seemingly, be different if the sign read "Buy your Milk at our Supermarket". In *Hill v Tupper* (1863), the tenant of land adjacent to a canal claimed as an easement the exclusive right to operate pleasure boats on the canal. This argument was rejected because the right was of benefit only to Mr Hill's pocket and not his land. It was merely a licence. It could not, moreover, be said to benefit a business carried on the dominant tenement because his business was instead carried out on the servient tenement (*i.e.* the canal);

(b) Although the dominant and servient tenements need not be adjoining, they must be sufficiently proximate for a practical benefit to be conferred: *Pugh v Savage* (1934). As Byles J. put it, "You cannot have a right of way over land in Kent appurtenant to an estate in London" (*Bailey v Stephens* (1862)). It might, however, be possible to have an easement to run horses on gallops at Epsom even though the business of training race horses is situated in Glasgow.

3. The dominant *and* servient tenement must not be owned and occupied by the same person. It is not possible to have an easement over one's own land because an easement is a right exercisable over the soil of another. Rights exercised by an owner over his own land are sometimes known as quasi-easements (see below). It is possible, however, that a landlord can acquire an easement over his tenant's land (and vice versa) because there is no common occupation: *Borman v Griffith* (1930).

4. The easement must be capable of forming the subject matter of a grant. This entails that:

(a) there must be a capable grantor and grantee: A problem can arise where a tenement is owned by a corporation which does not have the power to grant or receive easements. In such cases, the easement must fail;

(b) the right must be sufficiently definite that it could be granted by deed (*i.e.* it must be known what right is granted). A vague or inexact right cannot exist as an easement: *Hunter v Canary Wharf* (1997) (no right to a television signal). There is, therefore, no easement of privacy: *Browne v Flower* (1911). Similarly, there is no right to a view nor a right to the general flow of air (not being in a defined channel) over land: *Harris v De Pinna* (1886);

(c) the rights must be within the general nature of rights capable of existing as easements. The list of easements is not closed and, as admitted in *Dyce v Hay* (1852), must accommodate societal change. For example, there are relatively new easements to park a car (*Newman v Jones* (1982)) and to use an airfield (*Dowty Boulton Paul Ltd v Wolverhampton Corp. (No. 2)* (1976)). Nevertheless, as Lord Brougham put it in *Keppel v Bailey* (1834), "incidents of a novel kind cannot be devised at the fancy or caprice of any owner". Although the right may exhibit the other characteristics set out in *Re Ellenborough Park* (1968), it is likely that a new easement will *not* be recognised where:

  (i) it involves expenditure by the servient owner: *Rance v Elvin* (1983). The only exception to this rule is the easement to require the servient owner to fence his land: *Crow v Wood* (1971); or

 (ii) it is a negative right, *i.e.* a right to stop a neighbour from doing something on his own land. In *Phipps v Pears* (1965), it was held that there could be no easement affording protection from the weather. This was because it was a negative right. In *Hunter v Canary Wharf* (1997) the right to an uninterrupted television would have amounted to an undue restriction of the use of the servient land (essentially, it would have prevented building on prime development land); or

(iii) it involves exclusive or joint user. The approach is simple: an easement is a right over someone else's land and, if the right amounts to exclusive or joint use, it contradicts the ownership rights of the servient owner: *Copeland v Greenhalf* (1952). There the storage and repair of vehicles on a narrow strip of land was so excessive that it excluded the servient owner from the land and went well beyond the normal idea of an easement. Similarly, in *Grigsby v Melville* (1972) the right to store goods in a cellar was rejected as an easement because it would give an exclusive right of use. In *Hanina v Morland* (2000), the claim to the exclusive use of a roof terrace could not lie in grant and was not an easement. These cases amount to a positive claim to legal possession of the servient tenement. If the exclusive use is not permanent, however, the court must decide which side of the line the right falls. Although a right to use a lavatory will involve an element of exclusive use, in *Miller v Emcer* (1956) it was upheld as an easement. In *Ward v Kirkland* (1969) a right to enter on the servient land in order to repair a wall on the dominant land was an easement as it involved only a trace of exclusive use by the dominant owner. These rights are clearly of a non-possessory nature. Problems can arise, however, with the right to park a car. If the right is to park anywhere on the servient land, then that can properly be regarded as an easement. It is merely a claim to use and not to possession. If, however, it is a right to park in a particular parking bay then that might be too extensive to amount to an easement because of the total ouster of the servient owner.

THE CREATION OF EASEMENTS

A basic principle is that all easements will have their origin in a grant and most methods of acquisition are traceable to a grant whether real or fictitious. The following methods of acquisition exist:

1. Statute

Easements may be granted by local Acts of Parliament, for example, giving a right of support to a canal constructed under statute or by general Act of Parliament, giving rights in respect of cables, gas pipes, sewers, etc.

2. Express grant or reservation

A common way of creating easements is by way of express grant or reservation (sometimes called a "re-grant") by deed. A grant occurs where the servient owner grants a right over his own land, *e.g.* X sells off Blueacre to Y and in the conveyance grants to Y a right of way over Blackacre which is land retained by X. Conversely, a reservation arises where a vendor wishes to reserve an easement over the land sold, *e.g.* X sells off Blueacre to Y, but in the conveyance to Y reserves for himself a right of way over Blueacre for the benefit of Blackacre. The extent of the right is, of course, dependent upon how it is worded in the conveyance. No special words are necessary as long as the intention is clear. In case of ambiguity of meaning, the interpretation of a grant is against the vendor (as servient tenement owner). If it is a reservation which is uncertain, it will be interpreted in a manner which favours the vendor (as dominant tenement owner).

3. Implied grant or reservation

At this point, grants and reservations are treated very differently. Implied grants are based upon the notion that there shall be no derogation from grant and are more common that implied reservations: *Peckham v Ellison* (1998). This is because the onus is on the vendor to reserve an easement expressly in the conveyance: *Re Webb's Lease* (1951). It is important to appreciate that a reservation will be implied only in relation to an easement of necessity and a common intention easement. There are various types of implied easement:

(a) *easements of necessity* are implied only in what are called "land locked close" situations where it is necessary to imply an easement so that the dominant owner can gain access to the dominant tenement: *Pinnington v Gallard* (1853). For example, X sells part of his land to Y. There is no means of access to the part bought except over the land retained by X. In these circumstances, if the conveyance is silent, a right of way will be impliedly granted to Y because of necessity. Alternatively, if X sells off part of his land to Y and X cannot gain access to the part he retains without crossing the land sold to Y, a reservation will then be implied. In all cases, the implication hinges on necessity and not mere convenience. In *Manjang v Drammah* (1991), the Privy Council confirmed that an available access by water, even though less convenient than access across land, was sufficient to negative any implication of a right of way of necessity. An easement of necessity can be excluded by a contrary intention that has been clearly expressed: *Hillman v Rodgers* (1997). If the necessity ceases, the easement also ceases;

(b) *common intention easements* are implied to give effect to the
common intention of the parties. The intention must be
particular and definite. In *Wong v Beaumont Property Trust*
(1965), the landlord let cellars to the tenant who covenanted to use them as a restaurant and to comply with
health regulations. It later transpired that, in order to
comply with the regulations, the tenant had to install an
effective ventilation system. This could occur only if the
tenant was allowed to run ventilation shafts up the side of
the landlord's wall. The landlord refused the tenant's
request, but the court held that the tenant had an implied
easement to affix the shafts. In appropriate circumstances,
a common intention easement can be impliedly reserved;

(c) *the rule in Wheeldon v Burrows* (1879) is that, when a
vendor sells off part of his land, the purchaser will
acquire through implication, "all those continuous and
apparent . . . quasi-easements . . . which are necessary to
the reasonable enjoyment of the property granted, and
which have been and are at the time of the grant used by
the owners of the entirety for the benefit of the part
granted" (*per* Thesiger L.J.). The rule is based upon the
rule against derogation from grant. The rule, therefore,
concerns rights ("quasi-easements") which the owner
previously exercised over the land he retains for the
benefit of the part he has disposed of. These rights can be
elevated to proper easements (either legal or equitable) on
the dealing with the quasi-dominant tenement. The conditions necessary for a *Wheeldon v Burrows* easement to be
implied are:

  (i) there must be common ownership and occupation of
the entirety of the land prior to the rule being
triggered;

 (ii) the quasi-dominant tenement must be dealt with (*e.g.*
sold, leased, acquired by will or subject to a contract
to sell). Hence, the rule only applies to implied
grants and cannot be relied upon to justify an
implied reservation. The rule also applies if the
common owner deals with both parts simultaneously: *Swansborough v Coventry* (1832). The effect is as
if the owner had sold the dominant tenement and
retained the rest: *Schwann v Cotton* (1916);

(iii) it must be "continuous and apparent". Continuous
appears to mean permanent and together with
apparent implies that the right leaves an obvious and

permanent mark on the land itself or, at least, the right must be one that would be revealed by a careful inspection of the land. A rough track was sufficient in *Hansford v Jago* (1921). Other examples would include water flowing through visible pipes, windows enjoying light or a defined passageway;

(iv) the right must be reasonably necessary to the enjoyment of the land. It has never been authoritatively established whether this reference is an alternative to the right being "continuous and apparent" or whether both conditions must be satisfied. The traditional view appears to be that both must be satisfied: *Wheeler v J.J. Saunders* (1995). There a right of way was not implied because an alternative access to the property existed, it was not deemed necessary for the reasonable enjoyment of the land;

(v) the right must have been used by the common owner up to the time where the quasi-dominant tenement was dealt with. *Wheeldon v Burrows* does not operate to resurrect past rights;

(vi) there must be no contracting out of the operation of the rule.

(d) *section 62 of the LPA 1925* states that, subject to a contrary intention expressed in the conveyance, every conveyance of land passes all privileges, easements, rights and advantages appertaining or reputed to appertain to the land or part of it. This general word saving provision can have unexpected consequences. It not only transmits the benefit of existing easements to a purchaser of the dominant tenement, but it can also create new legal easements from, say, what was previously a revocable licence. In *Wright v Macadam* (1940), the permissive right to use a coal shed passed as a legal easement under s.62 on the grant of a new lease. An implied grant (but never a reservation) can arise under s.62 where:

(i) there is a conveyance of the dominant tenement. The term "conveyance" is defined in s.205 of the LPA and does not include a will, gift or contract. It also does not include oral tenancy: *Borman v Griffith* (1930);

(ii) prior to the conveyance, there was common ownership of the dominant tenements, but diversity of occupation: see Lord Wilberforce in *Sovmots Invest-*

ments v Secretary of State (1979). Some judges have, however, concluded that the requirement of diversity of occupation gives way when the right is continuous and apparent (see Peter Gibson L.J. in *P&S Platt Ltd v Crouch* (2003)). This is, therefore, an area of some uncertainty and it is better to canvas both approaches. Nevertheless, an insistence upon on diversity of occupation is attractive in that it keeps s.62 and the rule in *Wheeldon v Burrows* apart in mutually exclusive spheres. This is appealing both in terms of logic and symmetry and is line with the approach adopted by the House of Lords in the *Sovmots* case;

(iii) there is no contrary intention specified in the conveyance or contract which precedes it;

(iv) the right is one which existed at the time of the conveyance and is not a spent or past right. It must also be capable of being granted by the common owner: *Quicke v Chapman* (1903). The rule is that neither s.62 nor the rule in *Wheeldon v Burrows* can affect other landowners.

4. Prescription

This applies to easements acquired by presumed grant, *i.e.* where the law presumes from long enjoyment that the right had its lawful origin in a grant. A prescriptive right may be acquired either at common law, under the doctrine of lost modern grant or by virtue of the Prescription Act 1832. In each case the following common criteria must be established:

(a) The use is "as of right." This is explained in the maxim *nec per vim, nec clam, nec precario* which requires that the right has not been obtained by force or coercion, and that it is not secretive: *Union Lighterage Co. v London Graving* (1902). Neither must it be permissive in nature: *Gardner v Hodson's Kingston Brewery* (1903). In *Mills v Silver* (1990), for example, a prescriptive right to use a track was claimed. Successive owners had allowed usage of the track because of good neighbourliness and because usage had previously been regarded as insignificant. Nevertheless, the court held that there had been acquiescence in the use of the track, permission had never been sought and consequently the right had been established. In *Bridle v Ruby* (1988) a mistaken belief that a right of way had been legally acquired did not prevent a 22 year user becoming a right by prescription since it was still deemed to be "as of right". In *Jones v Price* (1992) it was held that there was no prescriptive easement even though a track had been used from 1926 to 1979 since the right to use it was originally acquired by permission and continued by tacit consent until permission was withdrawn in 1979.

(b) The user must be "continuous", as far as the nature of the right allows. User can be by successive owners of the dominant tenement: *Davis v Whitby* (1974). A right of way used precariously (blocked at irregular intervals) could not, however, develop into an easement: *Goldsmith v Burrow Construction Co. Ltd* (1987).

(c) The user must be by or on behalf of a fee simple owner against a fee simple owner. If a tenant acquires an easement against a third party he acquires it on behalf of the fee simple estate. If a tenant occupies the servient tenement, an easement cannot be acquired against it. If the user began against a fee simple owner, however, it does not make it invalid for prescriptive purposes if the land is later leased. Easements cannot be prescribed for by one tenant against another tenant of the same landlord: *Simmons v Dobson* (1991).

(d) An easement cannot be acquired by conduct which, when it took place, was prohibited by statute or was contrary to public policy: *Hanning v Top Deck Travel* (1993). This does not, however, extend to a use in breach of planning controls unless enforced by the planning authority: *Batchelor v Marlow* (2000).

Common law prescription

At common law, a grant was presumed if enjoyment dated from "time immemorial", *i.e.* 1189. To overcome obvious evidential difficulties, the courts adopted the stance that, if 20 years' user could be shown, it would be assumed that the right had been enjoyed since 1189. This presumption will be rebutted if it could be shown that, at any time since 1189, the right could not have existed. For example, a claim to a right of light to a building erected after that date would fail. Similarly, if could be shown that the dominant and servient tenements had been in common ownership since 1189, the presumption would not operate.

Lost modern grant

A mechanism to avoid the rigours of the common law rule was developed by the courts under the fiction of lost modern grant. If a claimant can show actual enjoyment for a period of 20 years, the court is prepared to pretend that there was once a grant that has now been lost: *Dalton v Angus* (1881). As the grant never actually existed, there is no need to furnish the court with any particulars of it. The claim may, however, be defeated if proof is given that during the entire period since user started there has been no person capable of granting easements: *Tehidy Minerals Ltd v Norman* (1971). Although most claims will now fall under the Prescription Act 1832, the doctrine of lost modern grant is still invoked: see *Mills v Silver* (1990).

The Prescription Act 1832

The object of this Act was to simplify the method of acquisition of easements by prescription, but it was a poor attempt. The Act has been subjected to repeated criticism and it is amazing that it still forms a central part of modern property law. The Act draws a basic distinction between easements of light and other types of easement.

Easements other than light. Section 2 provides that an easement can be claimed where it is "actually enjoyed by any person claiming right thereto without interruption for the full period of 20 years". It cannot be defeated by showing that the user began after 1189. It may, however, be defeated in other ways, for example, if it was secretive, permissive or forcible user. The law changes as regards actual enjoyment for 40 years. This extended user makes the right "absolute and indefeasible" unless enjoyed by express consent given by deed or writing. Several observations may be made:

(a) In each case, s.4 states that the period of years is the period immediately preceding some "suit or action wherein the claim . . . shall be brought into question", *i.e.* an action by the parties relating to trespass or nuisance or merely an application for a declaration;

(b) To constitute an interruption to a period, there must be some act which shows the easement is disputed, which lasts for a year and which has been "submitted to or acquiesced in" by the dominant owner. An interruption for 364 days being less than a year will not count: *Reilly v Orange* (1955). Where the dominant owner protests at the existence of an interruption, this appears to postpone the commencement of that interruption for a reasonable period of time: *Davies v Du Paver* (1953). Where the servient owner lodges a complaint with the dominant owner about the existence of a right, this can amount to an interruption. If, after the complaint has been made, the dominant owner then fails to communicate with the servient owner this might be construed as an acceptance of the interruption: *Dance v Triplow* (1992).

Easements of light. Section 3 provides that, where a right of light has been actually enjoyed for a full period of 20 years without interruption, the right becomes absolute and indefeasible, unless enjoyed by written consent or agreement. Oral permission will not defeat this claim. The following points emerge:

(a) The amount of light that a building is entitled to is that which is required for any ordinary purpose for which the building has been constructed or adapted: *Colls v Home and Colonial Stores Ltd* (1904);

(b) An interruption of a right of light may be effected by erecting an obstruction, or alternatively by registration of a local land charge to have effect as an obstruction under the Rights of Light Act 1959;

(c) A tenant may acquire an easement of light against another tenant of the same landlord. This is an exception to the rule that prescription can operate only between freeholders.

Protection against third parties

In unregistered land, an *equitable* easement can be registered as a class D(iii) land charge. If not registered, it will not be binding on a purchaser of a legal estate for money or money's worth. A *legal* easement is, however, a right *in rem* and binds the entire world. In *Ives v High* (1967), the Court of Appeal discerned an estoppel interest from what appeared to be an unregistered, equitable easement. This was a "justice driven" decision in that, as an estoppel cannot be protected under the Land Charges Act 1972, it was binding on the purchaser who here had actual notice of the right.

In registered land, the Land Registration Act 2002 allows both legal and equitable easements to be protected by the entry of a notice on the Charges Register at the Land Registry. Legal easements (but never equitable easements) can, however, be classified as rights that override registration and, therefore, might bind a purchaser without them appearing on the land register. This does not, however, protect all legal easements and (subject to certain transitional provisions: see Ch.5) the only ones that can override a registered disposition are those that:

(a) Are created by prescription or implication (thereby, excluding express grants and reservations); and

(b) Are in the actual knowledge of the purchaser or would have been obvious on a reasonable inspection of the servient property; or

(c) Where the right has been exercised during the calendar year leading up to the disposition.

Extinguishment of easements

Easements can be extinguished in several ways:

Abandonment

This can occur by either:

(a) *express release*: a deed is required at common law, but equity will assist a servient owner who, relying on an agreement to release, acts to his prejudice. This will give rise to an estoppel which will prevent the other party denying the non-existence of the easement;

(b) *implied release*: an intention to abandon must be shown, but non-user alone is inconclusive. Non-user for 175 years of a right of way granted in 1818 did not of itself indicate an intention to abandon it: *Benn v Hardinge* (1992);

(c) *practical impossibility*: a change of circumstances might make cause an easement to be extinguished. If there is no longer any practical possibility of the easement ever again benefiting the dominant tenement in the manner originally contemplated, the easement will lapse: *Huckvale v Aegean Hotels Ltd* (1989).

2. Unity of ownership and possession

Where the fee simple of both tenements become vested in the same owner, the easement will be extinguished. It is not possible to have an easement over one's own land. The easement will not be revived on any subsequent sale of one of the tenements.

3. Statute

An easement may be extinguished either expressly or by implication by Act of Parliament, for example, under the Commons Registration Act 1965.

10. MORTGAGES

Introduction

1. A mortgage (whether legal or equitable) is essentially a pledge of land (or other property) as security for the repayment of a loan.
2. The person who borrows the money is known as the *mortgagor* and the lender is the *mortgagee*.
3. The mortgagee is a secured creditor, acquires a property interest in the land and is in a much stronger position than an unsecured creditor. For example, on the mortgagor's bankruptcy the mortgagee's claim will prevail against other creditors. If the borrower defaults on, say, repayment, the lender has an extensive array of remedies which can be employed. The main remedy of the mortgagee is the power to sell the mortgaged property.
4. The borrower retains legal estate to the land and will remain in occupation of the property. The borrower has a right of redemption (*i.e.* to pay off the mortgage) at any time after the contractual date for redemption (see below). The borrower's rights under the mortgage are for simplicity often described as the mortgagor's *equity of redemption*: *Casborne v Scarfe* (1738).

CREATION OF MORTGAGES

1. Legal mortgages of unregistered land

   (a) By virtue of s.85(1) of the Law of Property Act 1925 legal mortgages of a *freehold* estate may be created in one of two ways:

(i) by a demise for a term of years absolute, subject to a provision for redemption. Any attempt to create a mortgage by conveyance of the freehold estate is to take effect as a lease for 3,000 years: s.85(2); or

(ii) by a charge by deed expressed to be by way of legal mortgage. The mortgagee has all the same protection, powers and remedies as if the mortgage had been created by the grant of a term of years: s.87(1). LPA.

(b) By virtue of s.86(1) of the LPA, legal mortgages of a leasehold estate can be created in two ways:

(i) by granting a sub-lease of a term of years absolute to the mortgagee subject to a provision for redemption; or

(ii) by a charge by deed expressed to be by way of legal mortgage.

2. Legal mortgages of registered land

A legal mortgage of registered land can now be created only by a charge expressed to be by way of legal mortgage: s.23(1)(a) of the Land Registration Act 2002. The mortgage, moreover, only becomes legal once it is registered as a charge at the Land Registry. Whether it is the freehold or leasehold estate that is the subject of the mortgage, it is no longer possible to have a mortgage by demise or sub-demise of registered land. This shift has occurred because a legal charge has some practical advantages over the other types of mortgage:

(a) it is convenient, less cumbersome and less expensive;
(b) it is easier to understand and explain to a purchaser;
(c) it does not infringe a provision (in a lease) against subletting.

3. Equitable mortgages

Equitable mortgages are rare, but will arise where:

(a) there is insufficient formality to create a legal mortgage, *i.e.* in the absence of a deed. An equitable mortgage will be created if, for example, the mortgage is merely in writing. If, however, it is in writing, and satisfies the other conditions of s.2 of the Law of Property (Miscellaneous

Provisions) Act 1989 (*i.e.* it is signed by both parties and contains all the express terms), it might amount to a valid contract to create a legal mortgage. The court may then award specific performance of this contract and direct that a deed be executed to overcome the informality. If there is no writing whatsoever then it cannot even exist as an equitable mortgage: s.53(1)(a) LPA;

(b) a mortgage of an equitable interest, and regardless of how it is created, must necessarily be equitable. For example, the mortgage of a life estate or a beneficial interest under a trust of land or strict settlement must, therefore, be an equitable mortgage. The lender will acquire the entire equitable interest, subject to a proviso for reassignment on full payment of the loan.

RIGHTS OF THE BORROWER

1. The right to redeem

Once a mortgage has been created, there will normally be a contractual date set for repayment of the loan; this is known as the *legal redemption date*. The date is often set six months from the date of the loan. Until this time, the borrower cannot (without the consent of the lender) redeem nor can the lender exercise some of its key remedies (*e.g.* sale). At common law, if the money was not paid on the precise date, the property automatically vested in the mortgagee. This was a harsh and unfair rule and so equity intervened and created an *equitable right to redeem*, *i.e.* equity gives the mortgagor the right to redeem the property once the legal redemption date has passed. This should not be confused with the *equity of redemption* (shorthand for the entire interest of the borrower under the mortgage). Equity is protective of the right to redeem. It is inviolable and cannot be excluded or rendered illusory:

(a) any provision preventing a mortgagor from recovering the property after redemption is repugnant to the nature of the transaction and void. It is said that there can be "no clog or fetter on the right to redeem." A provision in a mortgage that stipulates that property shall belong to the mortgagee on the occurrence of some event is, thereby, ineffective. Similarly an option to purchase contained in a mortgage deed is void: *Samual v Jarrah Timber* (1904). Such a provision runs in contradiction to the equitable right to redeem. If, however, the option is granted by the borrower in a separate and independent transaction, it can be upheld: *Reeve v Lisle* (1902);

(b) the right to redeem may, however, be restricted or modified. A provision postponing the date of redemption may be valid provided that it does not make the equitable right to redeem of no value. In *Fairclough v Swan Brewery Co. Ltd* (1912), a 20-year lease was mortgaged on conditions that prevented its redemption until six weeks before the end of the term. This was held to make the equitable right to redeem illusory and therefore void. By way of contrast, in *Knightsbridge Estates Trust Ltd v Byrne* (1939) it was held that, in the context of a mortgage of the freehold estate, a clause postponing redemption for 40 years was valid. It was significant that the parties were large commercial enterprises that had entered into a mutually enforceable agreement after being professionally advised. The key notion is that any postponement cannot be oppressive or unconscionable. Equity will not, however, rewrite a mortgage transaction simply because the postponement is unreasonable;

(c) a mortgage is subject to the common law rule that an agreement which operates as an unreasonable restraint of trade is void. For example, in *Esso Petroleum v Harper's Garage* (1968) an agreement which tied the borrower to selling only the products of the lender (sometimes called a "solus" agreement) for a period of 21 years was invalid. It appears that the court will uphold "solus" agreements that are limited to relatively short periods. In the same case, a tie in for five years was upheld;

(d) collateral advantages might be reserved in the mortgage in addition to the repayment of the loan and interest. These added or collateral obligations are permitted providing that they are not unconscionable and do not constitute a clog on the right to redeem:

(i) in *Noakes v Rice* (1902), the mortgagor of a public house agreed that he would sell only the lender's beer for the duration of a 26–year lease. The collateral advantage was void because it was oppressive. In *Biggs v Hoddinott* (1898), however, the mortgage agreement provided that the mortgage could not be redeemed for five years and that, during this period, the borrower would sell only the lender's products. The collateral advantage was upheld as being reasonable and fair.

(ii) as a general rule any collateral advantage must cease when the mortgage is redeemed: *Bradley v Carritt* (1903). In *Kreglinger v New Patagonia Meat and Cold Storage Co. Ltd* (1914), however, the House of Lords upheld a mortgage term which provided that, for a period of five years, the mortgagor could not sell any animal skins to anyone other than the mortgagee. Although the mortgage was paid off within three years, the collateral advantage was viewed as a distinct and independent agreement and as such capable of continuing in force after the mortgage had been redeemed. It was a bona fide business deal between the parties;

(iii) a clause in a mortgage which ties repayments by way of an index-linking arrangement to the value of the Swiss franc was not unconscionable even though it might require a substantial rise in interest repayments: *Multiservice Bookbinding Ltd v Marden* (1978). In *Cityland Holdings Ltd v Dabrah* (1968), however, an annual interest rate of 19 per cent (at a time when the national rate was 7 per cent) which was set to rise to 57 per cent on any default in repayment was an unconscionable collateral advantage and void.

2. The right to grant leases

By virtue of s.99 of the LPA, the mortgagor in possession can grant certain leases that will be binding on the mortgage lender. This power can, however, be excluded in the mortgage agreement and this is common practice. A mortgagee will not be bound by an unauthorised lease and the lender has an unqualified right to take possession as against an unauthorised tenant. A mortgagor also has a right to accept a surrender of a lease: s.100.

3. The right to be protected from extortionate credit bargains

The Consumer Credit Act 1974 gives the courts a power to reopen any extortionate credit agreement so as to do justice between the parties: ss.137–140. The court will look at interest rates, the debtor's personal attributes, financial pressures and the degree of risk accepted by the creditor together with other various factors likely to be material. The decision in *Ketley v Scott* (1981) illustrates the application of these provisions. Here the court refused relief where the mortgagor, an experienced businessman in receipt of legal advice, wanted to complete a house purchase the same day and agreed to pay an interest rate of 48 per cent. Similarly, in *Woodstead Finance Ltd v Petrou* (1985), an interest rate of 46 per cent was described as harsh, but was not designated "extortionate" because of "an appalling record of repayment". It is to be appreciated that the Unfair Contract Terms Act 1977 does not apply to mortgages. The Financial Services and Markets Act 2000, however, will (from October 31, 2005) impose a new code of conduct of mortgage lenders and introduce a principle of "responsible lending". It will also ensure that mortgage lenders do not levy exorbitant charges on their customers.

4. The right to be protected against undue influence

A bargain entered into as a result of undue influence or other equitable wrongdoing (*e.g.* misrepresentation or duress) on the mortgagor may be set aside as against both the wrongdoer and the mortgagee: *Barclays Bank v O'Brien* (1994). The undue influence can be from the mortgagee (albeit unlikely) or from a third party (usually a husband) dealing with the mortgagee. This area has been subject to considerable judicial interpretation in recent years and this has culminated in the decision of the House of Lords in *Royal Bank of Scotland Plc v Etridge (No.2)* (2001). The following features emerge:

(a) undue influence is an equitable defence that concentrates upon the manner in which the intention to enter a contract is produced. If the intention was produced by an unacceptable means, the law will not permit the transaction to stand;

(b) the judicial tendency is to divide undue influence into two bands: class 1 (actual) and class 2 (presumed). Actual undue influence requires affirmative proof that the wrongdoer has actually exerted undue influence on the complainant to enter into the transaction. If, however, a *prima facie* case is established by showing that there existed a relationship of trust and confidence between complainant and alleged wrongdoer, and that the transaction is so disadvantageous that it calls for explanation, then the onus is on the alleged wrongdoer to provide a satisfactory explanation;

(c) presumed undue influence depends upon their being some pre-existing relationship of trust and confidence of such a nature that it is fair, in the light of the transaction, to require the alleged wrongdoer to prove that the transaction was freely entered. This will arise only in certain close relationships (*e.g.* doctor/patient; solicitor/client; trustee/beneficiary; child/parent; and priest/worshipper). It does not, however, cover husband and wife. If a sufficiently close relationship exists, it gives rise to the irrebuttable presumption that the dominant party has influenced the other. There is, however, no presumption that wrongdoing has occurred. If the transaction on its face calls for explanation, the burden of proof shifts to the alleged wrongdoer to show that there was nothing undue about the influence exerted;

(d) a mortgage lender will be affected by the wrongdoing of another when the loan appears not to be to the benefit the complainant (*e.g.* where a wife puts at risk the matrimonial home in order to guarantee her husband's business debts). In such cases, the lender is put on inquiry that some wrongdoing may have occurred. If the expressed purpose of the loan is for the joint benefit of the husband and wife (*e.g.* to buy a car or a holiday home), there is nothing which can put the lender on inquiry;

(e) once put on inquiry, and before the transaction goes ahead, the lender is expected to take steps to protect itself and to ensure that the vulnerable party understands the risks of the proposed loan. These steps are to ensure that the vulnerable party obtains legal advice; that the adviser is given sufficient information in order to advise properly; and that the transaction only goes ahead once the adviser has confirmed that the advice has been given.

RIGHTS AND REMEDIES OF A MORTGAGEE

Where a mortgagor defaults under the terms of the mortgage the mortgagee is given various remedies. These include taking possession, sale, foreclosure, suing on the personal covenant to repay and the appointment of a receiver.

Possession

1. The mortgagee's right to take possession arises automatically at common law and is exercisable even if the mortgagor is not in default: *Four Maids Ltd v Dudley Marshall Properties Ltd* (1957). In practice, possession will be sought only if the mortgagor is in breach of the mortgage agreement. This is because the modern lender is interested in money and not in turning people out of their homes. In addition, a mortgagee who takes possession is under certain duties, for example, to keep the property in reasonable repair and to account strictly for any rents and profits received. If the mortgagee leases the property, the lender must get the best possible rent: *White v City of London Brewery* (1889).

2. Usually, a court order for possession will be necessary in order to shield the lender from criminal and civil liability. Such an order is not necessary, however, if the premises are unoccupied or when the borrower has left willingly (*Ropaigealach v Barclays Bank Plc* (1999)). On the lender's application for possession of a dwelling house, the court has a statutory discretion to adjourn the proceedings or to grant a stay of execution of any order: s.36 of the Administration of Justice Act 1970 (as amended by s.8 of the AJA 1973).

(a) This statutory discretion is available only if it seems likely that, within a reasonable time, the mortgagor will be able to pay any sums due or be able to remedy any other breach of the mortgage. In *Cheltenham & Gloucester Building Society v Norgan* (1996), the Court of Appeal set out much needed guidance as to how the discretion should be exercised. It established the working rule that a reasonable time will be the remaining years of the mortgage. The borrower is, however, expected to produce a detailed budget to convince the court that it is likely that the arrears will be paid off as well as meeting future payments as they fall due. If the new arrangement is broken, the courts are unlikely to give the borrower a second chance. The *Norgan* approach operates only when there is the ability to discharge the arrears on an instalment basis and when there is no negative equity. A negative equity arises when the property is worth less than the debt owed. In *Norgan* there were 13 years remaining on the mortgage, the house was worth £225,000 and the amount owed was £97,000. The lender's position was secure and the court could afford to be generous. In *Realkredit Danmark v Brookfield House* (2000), however, this was not the case and the court ordered immediate possession. There more than £2 million was owed, but the property was worth only £1.5 million. The lender's interests were in real jeopardy.

(b) A mortgagee in possession has the following powers:
   (i) to cut and sell timber: s.101 of the LPA;
   (ii) the same powers of leasing as a mortgagor: s.99(2);
   (iii) the same powers as a mortgagor to accept surrenders of leases: s.100(2).

Sale

At common law, there is no power of sale. A statutory power of sale is, however, given by the Law of Property Act 1925. The Act draws a distinction between when that power *arises* and when it becomes *exercisable*. Where the power of sale has arisen (s.101), the mortgagee can give a good title to a purchaser free from the equity of redemption even if the power has been irregularly exercised: s.104. Consequently, a purchaser need only verify that the power of sale has arisen and this can usually be done by inspection of the mortgage deed. If the power has not arisen, however, the purchaser will merely get an assignment of the benefit of the existing mortgage.

1. Under s.101 the power *arises*:

   (a) if it is not excluded in the mortgage deed. For obvious reasons, such exclusion would be rare;
   (b) when the mortgage is made by deed. This includes all legal mortgages, but excludes most equitable mortgages as they will usually be created informally; and
   (c) when the legal redemption date has passed, *i.e.* the date specified in the mortgage agreement as the redemption date. This is normally six months after the mortgage is created.

2. Under s.103, the power of sale becomes *exercisable* where:

   (a) notice requiring payment of the entire mortgage money has been served and this has not been complied with within three months. This refers to capital payments; or,

(b) some interest under the mortgage is two months in arrears and unpaid; or,
(c) there is a breach of some other mortgage covenant (*e.g.* to insure or to keep in repair).

3. The effect of a sale is to vest the whole estate of the mortgagor in the purchaser subject to any superior (or prior) mortgages. Although the selling mortgagee will receive the purchase money, s.105 provides that after sale the proceeds are to be held on trust and to be used to pay in declining order:

(a) any superior mortgages;
(b) the expenses of the sale;
(c) the principal, interest and costs of the selling lender's mortgage;
(d) any inferior mortgages; and,
(e) as regards the residue (if any), the mortgagor.

4. A mortgagee does not usually need a court order to execute sale and is not a trustee of the power of sale: *Nash v Eads* (1880). The mortgagee has an unfettered discretion to sell to achieve repayment of the debt owed: *Cuckmere Brick Co v Mutual Finance* (1971). The lender need not, therefore, delay sale until, say, planning permission is obtained or leases granted in order to obtain a better price: *Silven Properties v Royal Bank of Scotland* (2003). In *AIB Finance Ltd v Alsop* (1998), a post office had been closed by the borrower and the court held that there was no duty on the lender to sell the business as a going concern. The obligation is to take reasonable precautions to obtain a fair and true market value for the property in the condition it is in when sold. The mortgagee need not advertise the property or attempt to sell it by auction. The mortgagee must, however, act in good faith and cannot sell the property to itself (*Tse Kwong Lam v Wong Chit Sen* (1983)) or sell it quickly at a knock down price (*Palk v Mortgages Services Funding* (1993). Sale at an undervalue will not be interfered with in the absence of fraud, negligence or bad faith: *Cuckmere Brick Co. Ltd v Mutual Finance* (1971). The mortgagee does not owe the borrower a duty of care in tort, but instead owes a duty to account in equity: *Downsview Nominees Ltd v First City Corp* (1992). A mortgagor can specifically agree to a sale at less than market price and if this occurs the mortgagor will be estopped from asserting a sale at an undervalue: *Mercantile Credit Co. v Clarke* (1997).

Judicial sale

In addition to the statutory power given specifically to legal mortgagees, the court is afforded a general power to order sale at the instance of any "person interested": s.91 of the LPA. This may, for example, be as an alternative to foreclosure (see below): *Twentieth Century Banking v Wilkinson* (1977). It can also be employed by an equitable mortgagee or, indeed, by the borrower himself when the mortgagee will not agree to a private sale (*e.g.* there is a negative equity): *Cheltenham & Gloucester Building Society v Krausz* (1996). In *Palk v Mortgage Services Funding* (1993), the lender wished to lease the mortgaged property whereas the borrower wanted an outright sale. The borrower obtained a court order for sale under s.91.

Foreclosure

Foreclosure is the most draconian weapon in the armoury of the lender. It amounts to a total confiscation of the mortgagor's interest in the property. In a foreclosure action the court declares that the mortgagor's equitable right to redeem is extinguished and the mortgagee becomes owner at law and in equity. It disregards the fact that the property might be worth more than the debt outstanding and discounts any repayments made over previous years. Not surprisingly, the court is reluctant to order a foreclosure and will inevitably grant sale instead: *Palk v Mortgage Services Funding* (1993).

The most important features of foreclosure are:

1. The legal date for redemption must have passed (see above).
2. There must be a court order. The mortgagee must bring an action in the High Court and all parties interested must be made parties to the action (*e.g.* the borrower, any other mortgagees and any tenant of the mortgagor). The court will issue a foreclosure order *nisi*, which will require the mortgagor to repay what is due on or before a specified date (generally 6 months hence). In default the order is made *absolute*. This does not mean that it is final because foreclosure can be reopened by the court at any time in the future and the borrower's equity of redemption revived: *Campbell v Holyland* (1877).
3. In proceedings any "person interested", namely the mortgagor or subsequent mortgagee, may apply for judicial sale rather than foreclosure: s.91 LPA.

Appointment of a receiver

1. This is the appointment of a person or company with management powers who may collect rents and profits arising from the mortgaged land. Such a remedy is most commonly used where the mortgagor has leased the property and rents and profits can thereby be intercepted. The mortgage agreement will usually designate the receiver as the agent of the mortgagor, but this is no true agency. The mortgagor does not appoint the receiver, cannot give him instructions, cannot sack him, there exists no contractual relationship between them and the duties of the receiver are owed in equity to both the borrower and the lender: *Silven Properties Ltd v Royal Bank of Scotland* (2003). The receiver's primary function is to exercise his management powers to try and ensure that the debt is repaid, *i.e.* for the benefit of the lender. The receiver can, moreover, sell the property in the name of the mortgagor.

2. The power to appoint a receiver arises and is exercisable as with a power of sale and a mortgagee already in possession may appoint a receiver. Such appointment must normally be in writing: s.109 of the LPA.

3. The receiver must apply any income received in the following order:

   (a) payment of rent, rates and taxes;
   (b) payment of interest on any incumbrances having priority to the mortgage;
   (c) the receiver's commission, premiums and cost of repairs;
   (d) interest on the mortgage;
   (e) if the mortgagee so directs in writing, payment towards the discharge of the principal sum;
   (f) any surplus to the person next entitled (*e.g.* inferior mortgagees or the mortgagor).

4. The extent of a receiver's duty to the mortgagor was reviewed by the Court of Appeal in *Medforth v Blake* (1999). The court stated that, where a receiver manages property, his duties to the mortgagor and anyone else interested in the equity of redemption were not necessarily confined to a duty of good faith. Rather, in exercising a power of management the receiver owes a duty to manage the property with due diligence subject to a primary duty of attempting to create a situation where the interest on the secured debt could be paid and the debt itself

repaid. Due diligence does not necessarily oblige the receiver to continue a business at the mortgaged property nor, as a pre-requisite to sale, to obtain planning permission or to grant leases.

Right to sue on the personal covenant

1. As with any debt, the mortgagee can sue the borrower for the amount outstanding. The right to sue will be statute-barred after 12 years if the mortgage is created by deed (this is called a "specialty" debt). If the mortgage is not created by deed, the normal limitation period of six years operates.

2. The above remedies are in general cumulative; for example, if sale realises less than the mortgage debt then the mortgagee may sue on the personal covenant. Foreclosure, however, puts an end to the other remedies: *Cheltenham and Gloucester B.S. v Johnson & Sunshine* (1997).

Miscellaneous rights

1. The right to lease and accept surrenders: ss.99, 100 of the LPA.

2. The right to fixtures attached to the mortgage property (*i.e.* they become part of the security for the loan).

3. In unregistered land, the right to possession of the title deeds (ss.85, 86 of the LPA) and an obligation to redeliver them on redemption.

4. The right to insure the property: ss.101, 108 of the LPA.

5. The right to tack further advances. In certain circumstances a mortgagee may demand repayment of several loans in priority to lenders who made intervening loans. It is an amalgamation of one mortgage with another by the same lender of a higher priority. This is a method of leap-frogging the basic rules on priority of mortgages.

6. The right of consolidation. This applies where there are mortgages of more than one property held by the same lender. It is the right of a lender in whom two or more mortgages are vested to refuse to allow redemption of one without redemption of the others. The right will not exist unless the following conditions can be satisfied:

   (a) the right to consolidate must expressly be given in one of the mortgage deeds: s.93(1) LPA;

(b) the legal redemption dates on both mortgages must have passed;
(c) both mortgages must have been made by the same mortgagor;
(d) at some stage both mortgages must have been vested in one person and at the same time both equities of redemption were vested in another. This is termed the simultaneous union of mortgages and equities.

Equitable mortgagees

An equitable mortgagee has many of the rights and powers of a legal mortgagee, but there are some major differences:

1. Sale. Only if the mortgage is made by deed, does the equitable mortgagee enjoy the right to sell under s.101–103 of the LPA. Otherwise, the court may order a sale by virtue of its s.91 power.

2. Foreclosure. Equitable mortgagees may go for foreclosure because they do not generally have a power of sale in the knowledge that, instead, the court will order sale under s.91.

3. Possession. The equitable mortgagee has no right at law to possession because he holds no legal estate. If sale is ordered by the court, the court will also order that vacant possession be given. An equitable mortgagee cannot collect rents without a court order since he does not have the legal reversion.

4. Receiver. A statutory power under the LPA exists if the mortgage was made by deed. If no deed exists, the court also has an inherent power to make an appointment.

5. Sue on the personal covenant. The mortgagor can be sued personally for the recovery of the debt. If not by deed, there is a six year limitation period within which to commence proceedings for recovery of the debt.

Priority between mortgages

It is possible that there may be several mortgages charged on the same property. If there is a sufficient equity in the property to discharge all the loans then there is no major problem. All mortgages can be discharged from the proceeds of sale. Difficulties arise, of course, when there is insufficient money to achieve this (*i.e.* when there is a negative equity) and it then becomes crucial to know which lender has first (and perhaps second and third) bite at the proverbial cherry. This is known as priority. The rules governing priority differ according to whether title to the land is unregistered or registered.

1. Unregistered land

Priority here turns upon whether the mortgagee has title deeds to the property. The first mortgagee has the right to call for title deeds: ss.85, 86 of the LPA 1925.

(a) If the title deeds are in the physical custody of the lender, that lender always has priority over all others and this rule applies whether of not the prior mortgage is legal or equitable: s.97.

(b) As regards other mortgagees, s.97 provides that *legal* mortgages not protected by deposit of title deeds (so called "puisne" mortgages) rank in the chronological order in which they were protected by entry of a C(i) land charge.

(c) As regards *equitable* mortgages not protected by title deeds, those mortgages have to be protected by entry of a C(iii) land charge, but priority here is not governed by the order in which the land charges were entered. Instead, priority is governed by s.4 of the Land Charges Act 1972 which provides that, if an earlier mortgage has not been protected by a C(iii) land charge by the time the next mortgage is created, the earlier mortgage will be void as against the later mortgagee. This is so even if the earlier mortgage had entered a land charge before the later mortgagee enters his.

2. Registered land

Under the Land Registration Act 2002, a *legal* mortgage of registered land can now only be made by legal charge. *Equitable* mortgages can still be created informally. Under the 2002 Act, the following distinctions are drawn:

(a) once a *legal charge* is executed, it has to be entered on the Charges Register relating to the land. It is then called "a registered charge". The date of registration of the charge will be stated on the register. As to priority between registered charges, the rule is that the mortgages rank in the order in which they are entered on the Land Register. This is irrespective of the order of their creation;

(b) as regards other types of *legal* mortgage, they may be protected by entry of a notice on the Charges Register relating to the land. If so, it will take priority over a later mortgage whether that is a registered charge or an interest which is protected by notice on the Charges Register;

(c) in relation to *legal* mortgages which are not protected on the Charges Register and to *equitable* mortgages, the chronology of creation becomes important. The rule is that the earlier will prevail over the later. This is so even if the later is protected by a notice and the earlier is not. This rule does not, however, apply where the later mortgage is a registered charge. Section 30 of the 2002 Act provides that the registered charge will take priority over all unprotected mortgages.

11. LICENCES

Introduction

A licence is mere permission to be on land, that is, it prevents what would otherwise be an unlawful trespass: *Thomas v Sorrell* (1673). Licences, moreover, do not give the licensee a property interest: *Ashburn Anstalt v Arnold* (1989). Accordingly, a licence is not transferable and, being only a personal right, will not be enforceable against third parties: *Clore v Theatrical Properties* (1936). Licences fall to be distinguished from leases and easements.

TYPES OF LICENCE

There are several types of licence and these include:

Bare licences

Where the licensee provides no consideration it is called a bare or gratuitous licence and is revocable at any time on giving reasonable notice: *Re Hampstead Garden Suburb Institute* (1995). A bare licence would arise if you invite someone into your home for dinner or to stay overnight. Similarly, a bare licence would exist when you have free entry into a museum or art gallery. If the licensee refuses to leave, he becomes a trespasser and can be removed by reasonable force.

Contractual licences

This is a licence that is supported by consideration, *i.e.* it arises under the terms of a contract. Such a licence will emerge when you pay for admission to a cinema, concert venue or football ground. For example, when you enter a bar you are a bare licensee. At that stage, you can be asked to leave immediately (in the circumstances that would be reasonable notice) and there is nothing you can do. Once you order a drink, however, you become a contractual licensee. A contractual licence can be revoked in accordance with its terms or, if no mention is made of termination, on reasonable notice. Hence, the bar should allow you sufficient time to consume your beverage before asking you to leave. If not, you can (in theory) bring an action for breach of contract and will have a claim for compensation. In *Wood v Leadbitter* (1845) for example, damages were awarded to an individual who was ejected from a Doncaster race meeting. On occasion, however, the court may be willing to grant equitable remedies:

(a) In *Winter Garden Theatre (London) Ltd v Millenium Products Ltd* (1948), it was acknowledged by the House of Lords that an injunction might be used to preserve the sanctity of bargain underlying a contractual licence when it was an express or implied term that it could not be revoked. This approach cannot, however, protect a bare licensee since equity will not assist a volunteer;

(b) In *Verrall v Great Yarmouth B.C.* (1980), specific performance of a contract for the hire of a hall by the National Front was granted and the purported revocation by the local Conservative council, in breach of contract, was resisted. On the facts, damages were thought to be inadequate because the National Front would not have been able to find anywhere else to hold its two day conference. If sufficient notice had been give to the licensor, damages would presumably have been awarded instead. It seems that *Verrall* emphasises the consequences of the breach rather than the nature of the contractual licence itself. It is to be appreciated that, had the Council sold on the premises, the National Front would not have been able to enforce the contract against the purchaser: *King v David Allen & Sons* (1916).

Licences coupled with an interest

This type of arrangement arises where a licence is implied as ancillary to the grant of a property right, *e.g.* an easement or a *profit à prendre*. The right to hunt animals, fish, or cut timber may all imply a permission to enter on the land. As the property right is irrevocable, so must be the attendant licence. Hence, albeit indirectly, it has the potential to bind a purchaser as the shadow of the property right.

Licences protected by estoppel

1. At the core of an estoppel is the notion that some form of assurance (whether by words or conduct) has been made and detrimentally relied upon by the other party: *Willmott v Barber* (1880). Detrimental reliance can include monetary expenditure, the exertion of labour or bringing about a change of conduct or circumstances. The reliance must be reasonable and must be known (or should have been known) to the person making the assurance. In such situations, it would be unjust and uncon-scionable for the person making the assurance to rely upon his strict legal rights. Instead, that person is said to be "estopped" from resiling from that assurance. By extending the principle of estoppel to licences, the courts have introduced a new dynamic into the law. Hence, if an owner of land permits, promises or acquiesces in the use of land by another he may be estopped from denying that person's right to use the land. As an estoppel is a property right it can bind third parties and, in doing so, will protect the licence which it encases: *Ives v High* (1967).
2. The principle of proprietary estoppel has been applied to licences in a diverse range of situations. It is of a particular use because it can be used as a "sword' as well as a "shield," *i.e.* proprietary estoppel can be relied upon as a cause of action as well as a defence. This is illustrated by case law:

  (a) in *Dodsworth v Dodsworth* (1973), expenditure by a couple on improvements to a bungalow, after being encouraged and induced by an assurance that they could live there as their home for as long as they wished, created an estoppel allowing occupation until the expenditure had been reimbursed;

(b) in Pas*coe v Turner* (1979), a woman had lived with her lover in his house. He had assured her that on his death the house and everything in it would be hers. On the strength of this she expended money on repairs and improvements. An estoppel was created and, following his death, the court ordered that the property be conveyed to her;

(c) in *Inwards v Baker* (1965), a father encouraged his son to build a bungalow on his (the father's) land. The court held that the son had a right to occupy the land for as long as he wished;

(d) in *Crabb v Arun D.C.* (1976), an assurance was given that the claimant would be allowed a right of access across the defendant's land. In reliance on this statement, the claimant sold other land that would have provided an alternative access. The defendant was estopped from denying the right of access.

3. Once an estoppel has arisen, it is up to the court how it is to be satisfied. In many cases, this may simply mean giving effect to the assurance. The court is, however, unable to go beyond what was informally assured: *Orgee v Orgee* (1997). In each case, the court will order what it believes to be appropriate satisfaction having regard to the assurance and the reliance placed upon it. For example:

(a) by enforcing the terms of a contract or a lease previously agreed: *J.D. Developments Ltd v Quinn* (1992);

(b) by perfecting an oral gift, and ordering the transfer of title to the property: *Voyce v Voyce* (1991);

(c) by declaring one of two joint tenants to be the sole beneficial owner: *Lim Teng Huan v Ang Swee Chuan* (1992);

(d) by ordering a refund of the cost of any expenditure plus interest: *Burrows v Sharp* (1991).

Licences and constructive trusts

1. Although the use of estoppel is in current vogue, in a few cases the circumstances surrounding the creation of a contractual licence have, instead, given rise to an implied constructive

trust. In *Bannister v Bannister* (1948), an oral agreement allowing a woman to live rent free in a cottage for as long as she liked gave rise to a constructive trust. She had sold the property at an under value on the basis of this understanding. A similar style of case was *Re Sharpe* (1980) where an aunt lent money to her nephew on the understanding that she would live in his house for the remainder of her life. As with estoppel (see above), a constructive trust is itself a property right that can bind third parties and, when it clothes a contractual licence, can ensure that the licence also binds the purchaser.

2. In *Ashburn Anstalt v Arnold* (1988), it was emphasised that there is no general proposition that, when a person sells land and stipulates that the sale should be subject to a contractual licence, a constructive trust will be imposed upon the purchaser. The conscience of the estate owner must be affected in a way which gives rise to an obligation to meet the legitimate expectations of the third party: *IDC Group Ltd v Clark* (1992). In other words, there needs to be special circumstances showing that the transferee of the property undertakes a new liability to give effect to provisions for the benefit of third parties.

12. FREEHOLD COVENANTS

The rules governing the enforceability of leasehold covenants are considered in Ch.13. The rules affecting freehold covenants are, however, very different and must be kept distinct. This chapter is, therefore, concerned with the situation where one fee simple owner covenants in favour of another either positively (*e.g.* to construct or maintain a road) or negatively (*e.g.* not to build shops or conduct a certain business on his land). Although the covenants will be binding between the contracting parties, the major issue concerns the circumstances in which they will be enforceable by and against future purchasers. For example, A sells part of Whiteacre to B. A covenants in the conveyance that he will not build on the part retained. A later sells the retained land to C. B then sells his land to D. The central concern for D is whether he can enforce the covenant against C. As will become clear, the answer to this question lies in the law of restrictive covenants.

Original Parties

As between the original parties to the covenant there is privity
of contract and the original covenantee can enforce the express
covenant against the original covenantor. At common law only
parties to a deed could sue upon it, but this rule is now subject
to statutory qualifications:

1. Section 136 of the Law of Property Act 1925 permits the
benefit of a covenant to be expressly assigned in writing to some
other person. The assignee then stands in the shoes of the
assignor and can enforce the covenant in his own right. This
does not apply to the burden of a covenant.

2. Section 56(1) of the LPA provides that "a person may take an
immediate or other interest in land . . . or the benefit of any . . .
covenant . . . although he may not be named as a party to the
conveyance or other instrument". This allows enforcement by
persons other than a named party to the deed, provided such
persons are identifiable at the time of the deed: *Re Ecclesiastical
Commissioners for England's Conveyance* (1936). In order to be
within the ambit of s.56, a person must show that the covenant
was intended to benefit him, even though he was not a party to
the deed: *Beswick v Beswick* (1968). Consequently a reference to
successors in title is not enough for the purposes of s.56 as they
are not ascertainable at the time the covenant is created: *Kelsey v
Dodd* (1881). Once s.56 gives the benefit to an individual (who is
then treated as having been an original covenantee), the benefit
can then pass to his successors. This does not apply to the
burden of a covenant.

3. Section 1 of the Contracts (Rights of Third Parties) Act 1999
also permits someone other than the direct covenantee to
enforce the covenant. The 1999 Act applies where the covenant
identifies the third party either by name or as a member of a
class (*e.g.* successors in title). The third party need not be in
existence when the covenant is entered. This does not apply to
the burden of a covenant.

The Running of Covenants

When a covenant is enforceable by and against successors in
title of the original covenantor and covenantee, it is often said to
run with the land. This means that the benefit and burden of the
covenant are automatically transmitted when the respective
properties are sold off. In deciding whether a covenant runs

with the land there are two sets of principles: the common law rules and the equitable rules. Each must be examined separately. The common law rules should be applied first of all, as it is only if they are inapplicable that the equitable rules need be employed. The benefit and burden of both positive and negative covenants can pass at common law, but the equitable rules apply only to restrictive covenants: *Gafford v Graham* (1998).

1. Common law: the benefit

For the benefit of an express or negative covenant to pass at common law the following conditions must be satisfied:

(a) the covenant must *touch and concern* the land of the covenantee, *i.e.* the covenant must not be merely personal in nature. In *Smith v River Douglas Catchment Board* (1949), it was made clear that this requirement must either affect the land as regards mode of occupation or affect directly the value of the land;

(b) the covenantee must, at the time of the covenant, have a *legal* estate in land to be benefited. This is because equitable interests in land were not historically recognised by the common law courts. An assignee need not, however, have the same legal estate as the covenantee. In the *Smith* case, a tenant acquired the benefit of a covenant made with a predecessor in title who was a freeholder. It is not required that the covenantor have any estate in land;

(c) the covenant must have been made for the benefit of land owned by the original covenantee. No contrary intention should be expressed in the conveyance to the effect that the covenant was not intended to run with the land: *Rogers v Hosegood* (1900). In the absence of such contrary indication, s.78 of the LPA deems the covenant to have been made on behalf of successors in title.

2. Common law: the burden

The basic rule at common law is that the burden of a covenant (whether positive or negative in nature) *cannot* run with the land: *Austerberry v Oldham Corp* (1885). Consequently, only a person who is an actual party to the covenant can be sued at common law. Hence, if the original covenantor sells on the land the covenant could not be enforced against the new purchaser. The statutory relaxation of the privity of contract rules (*e.g.* under the Contracts (Rights of Third Parties) Act 1999) does not apply to the burden of a covenant.

3. Equity rules: the burden

The decision in *Tulk v Moxhay* (1848) allegedly fathered what is now known as the law of restrictive covenants. This enabled the burden of a negative covenant (but not the burden of a positive covenant: *Rhone v Stephens* (1994)) to run with the land. This could occur upon the satisfaction of certain conditions:

(a) the covenant must be negative in nature. For these purposes it is the substance and not the form or outward appearance of the covenant that is crucial. In *Tulk v Moxhay*, the covenant was to keep and maintain a garden in Leicester Square in an open state and uncovered by buildings. Although expressed in a positive voice (to do something), it was in reality a covenant not to do something (*i.e.* not to build) and, therefore, was a negative covenant. As a rule of thumb, if the covenant requires the expenditure of money in its performance (*e.g.* to maintain a roof) then it will be positive: *Haywood v Brunswick Permanent Benefit Building Society* (1888). A covenant which has both positive and negative elements can be severed so that the negative element will be binding on the land: *Shepherd Homes Ltd v Sandham (No. 2)* (1971);

(b) the covenant must be intended by the parties to benefit land retained by the covenantee. Subject to statutory modification, for the burden of a restrictive covenant to run there must be both a dominant and a servient tenement. If a covenantee does not own or retain adjacent land capable of benefiting from the restriction, the covenant is merely personal in nature and, as such, enforceable only between the original parties: *Formby v Barker* (1903). The primary object of the law of restrictive covenants is, therefore, to protect the enjoyment of the land to which the covenant relates: *London C.C. v Allen* (1914);

(c) the covenant must touch and concern the dominant land. This is a question of fact and physical proximity is a crucial factor in showing that the dominant land is benefited. In *Kelly v Barrett* (1924), it was stated that "covenants binding land in Hampstead will be too remote to benefit land in Clapham". The covenant itself must either affect the land as regards mode of occupation, or it must be such as to directly, and not merely from collateral circumstances, affect the value of the land: *Rogers v Hosegood* (1900). It has to be something more than personal convenience and advantage. In *Newton Abbot Co-op v Williamson & Treadgold Ltd* (1952), for example, a covenant designed to prevent trade competition was held to touch and concern as it benefited a trade carried out on the dominant land. As to what constitutes the dominant tenement, it was held in *Re Ballard's Conveyance* (1937) that the dominant tenement must be clearly identified. There the dominant tenement was the whole of an estate consisting of 1,700 acres and the covenant was held to be ineffective because it could not directly benefit the whole of that estate. If, however, a covenant is annexed expressly or impliedly to the "whole and each and every part" of the dominant land, it is enforceable by the successors in title to any part which actually benefits from it: *Robins v Berkeley Homes* (1996);

(d) the burden of the covenant must be intended to run with the land of the covenantor. Although this might be expressed or inferred from the wording of the covenant itself, s.79 of the LPA provides that, in the absence of a contrary intention expressed in the conveyance, a covenant is deemed to run with the land. The presumption is that the covenant was "made on behalf of the covenantor on behalf of himself his successors in title and the persons deriving title under him or them". As to the operation of s.79:

(i) Lord Upjohn in *Tophams Ltd v Earl of Sefton* (1967) explained that s.79, ". . . does no more than render it unnecessary in the description of the parties to the conveyance to add after the respondent's name: his executors, administrators and assigns";

(ii) in *Morrells of Oxford Ltd v Oxford United FC Ltd* (2001), the covenant was given by the City Council to the predecessor in title of Morrells of Oxford. The covenant prevented the City Council permitting any land within a half mile radius of the dominant tenement being used as a brewery, club or licensed premises. Oxford United bought land from the City

Council within this radius and, as part of its stadium development, wanted to open a hotel and sell alcohol from various outlets. It was clear that, unless s.79 operated, the covenant would be merely personal as it made no mention of successors in title. Morrells of Oxford attempted to rely upon s.79, but the Court of Appeal held that a contrary intention existed which prevented such reliance. The obstacle was that the conveyance had adopted an inconsistency of style between the drafting of landlord's covenants and tenant's covenants. The tenant's covenants were expressly made to bind future tenants whereas, as noted, the landlord's covenants were not. This contrast demonstrated an intention to exclude s.79 and, therefore, could not bind Oxford United FC Ltd.

(e) It must also be remembered that, for a restrictive covenant actually to bind a purchaser of the servient land, the general rule is that it must be registered. In unregistered land, this is done by the entry of a D(ii) land charge as regards covenants created after 1925. In relation to pre-1926 covenants, they are still subject to the doctrine of notice which means that, because they are necessarily equitable interests, they bind everyone except a bona fide purchaser of the legal estate for value without notice. Under the Land Registration Act 2002, restrictive covenants are burdens on registered land and must be protected by the entry of a notice on the Charges Register.

Equity rules: the benefit

It is, perhaps, a subject of initial confusion that there are two sets of rules (albeit similar) relating to the benefit of covenants: common law rules (see above) and equitable rules (now to be considered). The real distinction is that, with negative covenants, the remedy sought by the dominant owner will be an *injunction* preventing breach by the servient owner. As this is an equitable remedy, it is necessary to show that the conditions of equity as to benefit are satisfied. In addition, the equitable rules must always operate when the servient tenement has been sold on. The straightforward rule is, therefore, that the burden of covenant is unenforceable in equity unless the benefit of the covenant has run to the purchaser in equity: *J Sainsbury Ltd v Enfield LBC* (1989). The benefit can pass in one of several ways: annexation, assignment and under a building scheme:

(a) *express annexation* is the linking of the covenant to the benefited land and is achieved by express words in the covenant itself. Once the benefit is annexed it runs with the land automatically even if the successor to the land does not know it exists when he takes the conveyance. In *Rogers v Hosegood* (1900), express annexation occurred due to the use of the following words, "his successors and assigns and others claiming under him or them to all or any of his land adjoining . . . the said premises". It is, however, crucial that the benefited land be referred to because, without this identification, there can be no annexation. This means that a covenant merely with the "vendors, their heirs, executors, administrators and assigns" is insufficient for there is no reference to any land. A successor to a part of land must show that the benefit is annexed to that part: *Formby v Barker* (1903). In *Re Ballard's Conveyance* (1937), it was accepted that there can be no annexation if the area of the dominant tenement is greater than can be reasonably benefited. Accordingly, it is better practice to annex the covenant to the whole and to each and every part of the dominant tenement: *Zetland v Driver* (1939);

(b) *statutory or implied annexation* is catered for by s.78 of the LPA and this facility goes some way to overcome the problems of annexation by express words in the conveyance. Section 78 states that, "a covenant relating to any land of the covenantee shall be deemed to be made with the covenantee, and his successors in title and the persons deriving title under him or them, and shall have effect as if such successors and other persons were expressed." The provision dispenses with the need for express words. In *Federation Homes Ltd v Mill Lodge Properties Ltd* (1980), it was held that the purpose of s.78 was to effect annexation to the land as a whole and to each and every part. In *Roake v Chadha* (1983), it was made clear that the intentions of the parties remain relevant and, even though there is no express mention of this in s.78 (c/f s.79), that the presumption yields to a contrary intention. This means that, where the covenant is not qualified in any way, annexation will readily be inferred. If, however, the covenant expressly precludes the benefit from passing then s.78 can have no application. This reflects a sensible interpretation of s.78;

(c) *express assignment* of the covenant is a means of transmitting the benefit to a new purchaser of the dominant land. The assignment must, however, be coupled with a transfer of the land and the conveyance and the assignment must be simultaneous: *Miles v Easter* (1933). It is, therefore, possible for an unbroken chain of assignments to be built up with a new link arising on each sale of the dominant land. There is some force in the argument that, on a post-1925 break in the chain of assignment, s.78 will then operate to statutorily annex the covenant to the land. The difficulty with this "delayed annexation" argument is that, akin to *Morrells of Oxford Ltd v Oxford United FC Ltd* (2001), the original decision to assign might evince a contrary intention to displace the presumption of annexation;

(d) *a scheme of development or building scheme* can operate to pass the benefit of a covenant. Such a scheme will arise where an area of land is developed and the developer subdivides the land into plots and sells those plots to different purchasers. The developer may require each purchaser to enter into a number of covenants to maintain the quality of the estate. Where such a scheme subsists, the purchaser or his assignees can sue and be sued on the mutual obligations. Such a scheme creates a "local law" binding on all owners, irrespective of when the various plots were sold. Equity takes the view that the covenants can be enforced by all owners of land within the scheme. The following principles for the existence of a scheme were laid down in *Elliston v Reacher* (1908):

  (i) both parties must derive title under a common vendor;

  (ii) the common vendor must have, before selling to either party, laid out the estate, or defined parts thereof, for sale in lots subject to restrictions intended to be imposed on all the lots and which, though varying from lot to lot, are consistent only with a general scheme of development;

  (iii) the restrictions were intended by the common vendor to be and were for the benefit of all the lots intended to be sold; and,

  (iv) the parties to the action, or their predecessors in title purchased their lots from a common vendor on the footing that the restrictions were for the benefit of the other lots in the general scheme: see *Re Wembley Park Estate* (1968).

In more recent times, there has been some retreat from these formal requirements. The courts are more concerned with the identification of the area to be the subject of the scheme and that the intention was that a scheme of mutually enforceable obligations exist. In *Re Dolphin's Conveyance* (1970), for example, a scheme was held to exist even though there was no common vendor (there were several vendors). Similarly in *Baxter v Four Oaks Properties Ltd* (1965), a scheme was held to exist even though the common vendor had not laid out the estate in lots prior to the sale. Nevertheless, it is necessary that the existence of the scheme must be brought to the knowledge the prospective purchasers: *Emile Elias & Co. Ltd v Pine Groves Ltd* (1993). The general principles governing schemes apply also to sub-schemes, *i.e.* where a lot is subsequently sub-divided. Here the covenants are enforceable, as far as they are applicable, even though none of the purchasers themselves actually covenanted.

TREATING POSITIVE COVENANTS DIFFERENTLY

Although the *benefit* of positive freehold covenants can run with the dominant land, it has been long established that the *burden* of a positive freehold covenant cannot: *Austerberry v Oldham Corp* (1885). This rule has been criticised by the Law Commission in 1965, 1971 and, for good measure, in 1984. Nevertheless, the rule has recently been affirmed by the House of Lords in *Rhone v Stephens* (1994). Equity, as Lord Templeman explained, ". . . has no power to enforce positive covenants against successors in title of the land. To enforce such a positive covenant would be to enforce a personal obligation against a person who has not covenanted." Accordingly, equity views a negative covenant as merely depriving an owner of rights that would otherwise have existed. It views positive covenants, however, as being outside the policing of equity because to compel a subsequent owner to comply with such a covenant would contradict the common law rule as to privity of contract. As Lord Templeman continued, "Enforcement of a positive covenant lies in contract; a positive covenant compels an owner to exercise his rights. Enforcement of a negative covenant lies in property; a negative covenant deprives the owner of a right over property."

2. In 1984, the Law Commission advocated the creation of *land obligations* which would amount to a new interest in land and would embrace both negative and positive freehold covenants. These were intended to include *neighbour* obligations (*i.e.* covenants between individuals) and *development* obligations (*i.e.* part of a development scheme). The technical rules considered above would be replaced by a simple rule that the benefit and the burden (if registered) would thereafter run. Unfortunately, and like many other Law Commission recommendations, these proposals are unlikely ever to become law. There are, however, several ways in which the rule, preventing the burden of a positive covenant binding third parties, can be sidestepped.

Circumventing the rule

At present, it is possible to circumvent the rule in *Rhone v Stephens* and this can be achieved by:

(a) granting a lease. Developers might want to sell off plots on a leasehold basis because (as shown in Ch.13) the burden of both negative and positive leasehold covenants run with the land due to the concept of privity of estate;

(b) setting up a commonhold scheme. Under the Commonhold and Leasehold Reform Act 2002, a developer can create a commonhold scheme, say, of a block flats. This a new type of freehold title which is specifically designed so that the burden of positive covenants can run with the land;

(c) maintaining a chain of indemnity covenants. If the original covenantor and each successor in title of the servient tenement obtains an indemnity covenant from the next purchaser, the continuing liability of the original covenantor can be offset by a claim for indemnity. This is a cumbersome and unreliable method of passing on responsibility because the system will break down if there is a break in the chain of indemnities;

(d) the benefit and burden rule. This prevents a claim to the benefit of a covenant without performing the burden and can be employed to enable the burden of a positive covenant to bind a third party. This is sometimes known as the rule in *Halsall v Brizell* (1957). This means that, if a person wishes to take advantage of a service of facility (*e.g.* to use a road or drains), he must comply with any consequential obligation that goes with it (*e.g.* contributing to the maintenance of the road or drains). As in *Shiloh Spinners Ltd v Harding* (1973), this will make the otherwise unenforceable positive covenant enforceable against a new purchaser. This mutual benefit and burden rule was applied in *Tito v Waddell (No. 2)* (1977), where the successors in title of a mining company who had acquired rights to remove phosphate from the land (the benefit) had to replant the land with indigenous trees and shrubs (perform the burden). In *Allied London Industrial Properties Ltd v Castleguard Properties Ltd* (1997), it was argued that, in order to take advantage of a right of way over a road, the purchaser must comply with the positive obligations imposed by a related covenant to carry out road widening. It was held to be outside the benefit and burden rule because the positive covenant was not viewed as a condition of the exercise of the right of way. There was insufficient reciprocity between the right and the covenant. In *Thamesmead Town Ltd v Allotey* (1998), the use of a communal space and footpaths was enjoyed by two tenants in the Council overspill estate. The tenants acquired the freehold in their homes and were required to make a contribution towards the upkeep of the communal land. The court held that the tenants were free to choose whether to use the rights or not and, if they chose not to, did not have to contribute to the upkeep;

(e) enlargement of a long lease into a freehold estate. The resulting fee simple is made subject to all the same covenants and obligations as the lease would have been subject to had it not been enlarged: s.153 of the LPA. Positive covenants contained in the lease should, thereby, continue to bind despite of the change to a freehold estate;

(f) creating an estate rentcharge. This is made subject to the performance of positive obligations (*e.g.* to repair or to build). A rentcharge is an annual payment of money charged on the land which can been enforced if the money is not paid. A rentcharge to enforce the performance of positive obligations has survived abolition by the Rentcharges Act 1977.

Discharge of restrictive covenants

1. It is possible to determine the validity of a restrictive covenant by application to the court for a declaration as to its effect: s.84(2) of the LPA, as amended.

2. A restrictive covenant is permanently discharged where the dominant and servient tenements come into common ownership: *Texaco Antilles Ltd v Kernochan* (1973).
3. A restrictive covenant may be discharged on application to the Lands Tribunal under s.84(1) of the LPA. In making any order, the Lands Tribunal will take into account any development plan and planning policy for the area. Each application is considered on its facts: *University of Westminster v President of the Lands Tribunal* (1998). The Lands Tribunal may make a discharge order wherever:

(a) the restriction is deemed obsolete by virtue of changes in the character of the property or neighbourhood or other material circumstances: see *Re Bradley Clare Estates Ltd* (1987); or
(b) the continued existence of the covenant would impede some reasonable user of the land for public or private purposes, and either the covenant confers no practical benefit of substantial value or compensation would be adequate to cover any loss: see *Gilbert v Spoor* (1983); or
(c) the parties entitled to the benefit of the restriction have expressly or impliedly agreed to its discharge or modification. The parties must be of full age and capacity; or
(d) the proposed discharge or modification will not injure the persons entitled to the benefit of the restriction: see *Moody v Vercan* (1991).

13. LEASEHOLD COVENANTS

Introduction

The covenants lie at the core of the landlord and tenant relationship. They state the rights and obligations of the parties under the lease. Covenants can be positive in nature (*i.e.* they can compel a party to do something, for example, to pay rent and to insure) or they can be negative (*i.e.* they can restrict a party from doing something, for example, using the premises for business purposes). Both parties usually enter into a series of express covenants (*i.e.* explicitly stated in the lease) whereas other covenants may be implied by law.

Examples of express covenants

The express covenants that may be found in leases are varied and numerous with the tenant tending to give the majority of them. Most commonly, the landlord covenants to give quiet enjoyment (this is implied anyway) and, depending on the type of lease and premises, to keep the property in repair. The tenant usually covenants to pay rent and rates, not to assign without the landlord's consent, to insure and, where the landlord does not so covenant, to repair the property.

1. Covenants to repair

(a) The meaning of the word "repair" is not clear-cut and the wording of a covenant to repair often varies, *e.g.* to keep in "good tenantable repair"; "substantial repair"; or "perfect repair". In *Proudfoot v Hart* (1890), however, these descriptive labels were viewed as merely indicating such repair as, having regard to the age, character and locality of the house, would make it reasonably fit for occupation. The meaning of a covenant is construed as at the time it was granted. Particularly with old buildings, renewal of subsidiary parts might be involved in "repair", but not complete reconstruction: *Brew Bros v Snax* (1970). A covenant which required the landlord to keep the building in "good and tenantable condition" was wide enough to require him to put it into that condition: *Credit Suisse v Beegas Nominees Ltd* (1994). A covenant to "keep premises in repair" obliges the covenantor to keep them in repair at all times. A tenant will, therefore, be in breach immediately a defect occurs. A landlord will be in breach only when he knows of the disrepair and has failed to carry out remedial work within a reasonable time: *British Telecommunications v Sun Life Assurance Society* (1995).

(b) The covenant to repair may contain an exception for "fair wear and tear" which exonerates the covenantor from disrepair arising from the ravages of normal use and normal ageing. However, the covenantor is obliged to take action to prevent fair wear and tear causing other damage to the premises: *Haskell v Marlow* (1928).

(c) The normal remedy for breach of a covenant to repair is damages, although in exceptional cases specific performance may be granted. *Jeune v Queens Cross Properties Ltd* (1974). In terms of damages, the quantum cannot exceed the diminution in the value of the reversion, and no damages can be recovered where the premises are to be demolished or structurally altered so as to make repairs valueless at or soon after the end of the term: s.18(1) of the Landlord and Tenant Act 1927. A claim for the cost of alternative accommodation while the premises are uninhabitable is permissible: *Calabar v Stitcher* (1984).

2. Covenant against assigning sub-letting or parting with possession

(a) In the absence of any express provision in a lease, a tenant may transfer the property freely by way of assignment, sub-lease or otherwise. Any express provision in the lease will be strictly construed against the tenant: *Marks v Warren* (1979). In *Field v Barkworth* (1986) a covenant not to assign or underlet *any part* of the premises was broken by an assignment of the whole. In general, a covenant should expressly prohibit assignment, underletting and parting with possession of the whole or any part or parts of the premises.

(b) The form of the covenant may be "absolute" or "qualified". Subject to its relaxation by the landlord, an absolute prohibition is enforceable as it stands. A qualified covenant, however, prohibits assignment without the consent of the landlord. Pursuant to s.19(1)(a) of the Landlord and Tenant Act 1927, this consent cannot be unreasonably withheld. A tenant must, however, request consent before he can rely on s.19(1). If consent is withheld, the landlord should notify the tenant in writing and provide reasons: *Footwear Corporation Ltd v Amplight Properties Ltd* (1999).

(c) Under s.1(1) of the Landlord and Tenant Act 1988, a statutory duty is imposed upon a landlord to make a decision (once consent is requested under a qualified covenant) within a reasonable time of the tenant's application. If the landlord's consent is sought in writing, the burden of proof is shifted to the landlord to show that the consent has not been refused unreasonably. If consent has been unreasonably refused, the landlord commits a tort that will entitle the tenant to obtain damages or an injunction.

(d) The issue of "reasonableness" was considered in *International Drilling Fluids Ltd v Louisville Investments (Uxbridge) Ltd* (1985). There it was accepted that the landlord could refuse consent only on grounds which had to do with the relationship of landlord and tenant and the subject matter of the lease. The court will proceed in a commonsense manner and decide the issue, on an objective basis, on the facts of a particular case. For example, a landlord might be able reasonably to refuse consent if the proposed assignment would result in a diminution in the rental value of the premises: *Norwich Union Life Assurance Society v Shopmoor Ltd* (1999). As a general rule, it will be unreasonable to withhold consent based upon colour, race, nationality or ethnic or national origins (Race Relations Act 1976) or gender (Sexual Discrimination Act 1975).

(e) Section 22 of the Landlord and Tenant (Covenants) Act 1995 applies to qualified covenants against assignment of leases of commercial (not residential or agricultural) premises. This provides that a landlord may reasonably withhold consent to any assignment (not sub-letting or parting with possession) where the circumstances in which he may do so have been set out in an agreement and the circumstances anticipated in the agreement exist. The landlord can, therefore, stipulate in advance the circumstances in which he will refuse consent to the assignment of a tenancy. The landlord may, for example, impose conditions about future guarantees or criteria for assessing the creditworthiness of any proposed assignee. Any veto will automatically be reasonable if within the terms of the agreement.

Implied obligations of the landlord

1. Covenant for quiet enjoyment. The tenant has a right to possession at the commencement of the lease and is entitled to damages if his enjoyment is substantially interfered with by acts of the landlord. Examples of such acts usually take the form of direct physical interference such as disconnecting gas or electricity supplies or disturbance caused by noise or building works: *Southwalk LBC v Mills* (1998). Insulting and violent behaviour may also amount to a breach: *Sampson v Floyd* (1989).

2. Non-derogatation from grant. The landlord must not frustrate the use of the land for the purpose for which it was let. For example, if a building is leased for business purposes the landlord cannot do anything which undermines that purpose, for example, blocking the entrance to the tenant's premises: *Owen v Gadd* (1956).

3. Repair and fitness for habitation. At common law, there is no general guarantee that the premises let are fit for habitation nor is the landlord under an obligation to repair. Nevertheless certain exceptions to this rule exist:

(a) furnished dwelling-houses: must be reasonably fit for human habitation when let: *Smith v Marrable* (1843) (which concerned bug-infested premises);

(b) houses let at a low rent: under ss.8–10 of the Landlord and Tenant Act 1985 there is implied an obligation that the landlord will keep premises fit for human habitation throughout the tenancy;

(c) lettings of a dwelling-house for less than seven years: under ss.11–16 of the Landlord and Tenant Act 1985 the landlord must keep in repair the structure and exterior of the dwelling house, including drains, pipes and gutters and also keep in repair and proper working order the installations in the house (*e.g.* for water, gas, electricity, sanitation and heating purposes). In *Staves & Staves v Leeds C.C.* (1991) it was held that dampness in plasterwork was part of the structure and exterior. The landlord was liable despite the fact that the saturation of the plasterwork resulted from an inherent, building defect. A landlord is not, however, liable for inherent defects if their remedy would amount to improvements to the property;

(d) blocks of flats: if a landlord retains control of the means of access such as lifts and staircases, then he is under an obligation to keep them in repair: *Liverpool Corp. v Irwin* (1977);

(e) defective premises: under s.4 of the Defective Premises Act 1972 the landlord is obliged to take reasonable care to ensure that persons who might be affected by defects in the premises are reasonably safe from injury or damage. In *Wallace v Manchester C.C.* (1998) the obligation was breached by a landlord who permitted a collapsed wall, rotten windows, a failed damp proof course, loose plaster and skirting, rat infestation and leaking rainwater pipes.

Implied obligations of a tenant

(a) not to commit waste: a tenant will usually be liable for both voluntary and permissive waste and so must keep the premises in repair: *Warren v Kean* (1954);

(b) to pay rent: this is payable in arrear and remains payable even if the premises later become unusable by the tenant (*e.g.* they are damaged by fire);

(c) to pay rates and taxes: this rule gives way if Parliament imposes a tax to be paid by the landlord;

(d) to allow the landlord to enter and view: this is implied where the landlord has covenanted to repair.

The usual covenants

Albeit rare, a contract and/or the lease itself might be expressed to contain the "usual covenants" without detailing further what they are. Although what is "usual" may vary according to the nature of the premises, their location and the purpose for which they are let, they will include the following covenants:

(a) to pay rent;
(b) to pay tenant's rates and taxes;
(c) to keep and deliver up in repair;
(d) to permit the landlord to view the state of repair;
(e) a forfeiture clause which will allow the landlord re-entry on non-payment of rent by the tenant.

ENFORCEMENT OF LEASEHOLD COVENANTS

This area of the law has undergone significant changes by virtue of the Landlord and Tenant (Covenants) Act 1995. The Act became operative on January 1, 1996 and its most significant provisions apply to leases that are created on or after that date. It is necessary, therefore, to know both the old and the new rules as to enforceability. It will become clear that for a covenant to be enforced the either privity of contract or privity of estate must exist between the parties.

Rules for leases created before 1996

1. Privity of contract

(a) as between the covenanting parties the position is simple: each party can sue the other for breach of contract. The rule is that, as the covenants survive for the duration of the lease, the potential liability of these parties lasts until the lease ends;

(b) on assignment of the lease by the original tenant, the original tenant still remains liable on the covenants and can still be sued by the original landlord. The original tenant can, therefore, be liable for breaches committed by any future assignee of the tenancy. Similarly, if the original landlord assigns the reversion, the original land-lord remains liable to the original tenant for breaches committed by his assignee;

(c) the landlord has an option of suing the original tenant (privity of contract) or the tenant for the time being (privity of estate: see below). The tenant for the time being is the principal debtor and the original tenant is the surety. It is up to the landlord to decide whom to sue. A similar choice is available for the original tenant who seeks to sue for breach of landlord's covenant by an assignee of the reversion;

(d) Although an original party can be sued following an assignment of his interest, on assignment the original party loses the right to sue for future breaches of cove-nant: *Re King* (1963). This is no hardship for the assignor because he will have suffered no loss as a result of the subsequent breach. As regards pre-assignment breaches, however, it was held in *City & Metropolitan Properties v Greycroft* (1987) that a former tenant can sue the landlord for a loss that occurred while he was a tenant, even though the lease has since been assigned. The same rule does not, however, apply to former landlords (see below);

(e) where the original tenant creates a sub-tenancy, the tenant remains liable for breaches of covenant in the main lease even though the fault lies with the sub-tenant. There is no direct relationship of privity of contract or estate between a head landlord and a sub-tenant so that as a general rule neither can sue the other directly;

(f) the right to sue the original tenant for pre-assignment breaches of covenant passes automatically to the new landlord under s.141 of the LPA without the need for an express transfer of the benefit of the contract. For this purpose alone, privity of contract exists between the new landlord and the original tenant: *London and County (A & D) Ltd v Wilfred Sportsman Ltd* (1971).

2. Privity of estate

In order to make the leasehold system work, the covenants have to be made binding on third parties (*i.e.* assignees of the landlord and tenant). This is achieved by a concept known as "privity of estate":

(a) this entails that the covenants become imprinted on the estate and are always enforceable by and against the current landlord and the current tenant: *City of London Corporation v Fell* (1994). This is necessary as the contractual relationship exists only between the original parties and they may die or become insolvent many years before the end of the lease;

(b) privity of estate exists independently from, and parallel to, the contract which created the covenant. If an original tenant is released from liability, this leaves unaffected the liability of the current tenant;

(c) an assignee is only liable whilst he holds the lease or reversion and after that time there is no longer any privity of estate (or, indeed, contract) between the parties;

(d) assignees are only bound by covenants which "touch and concern the land" (*i.e.* a covenant that is referable to the land and not merely a personal covenant: ss.141, 142 of the LPA 1925). This is known as the rule in *Spencer's* case (1583). Covenants by the tenant to pay rent or repair would "touch and concern" the land, but a covenant to pay rates on other land would not. A covenant by the landlord to renew the lease would "touch and concern", but not a covenant to sell the reversion at a stated price at the tenants' option. A covenant does not "touch and concern" merely because its breach may cause forfeiture of the lease.

3. Examples:

   (i) L grants a lease to T for 20 years. For the duration of the lease, L and T are in privity of contract with one another which means that they can sue each other for breaches of covenant;

  (ii) If T assigns the lease to A. As privity of contract still exists between L & T, L can sue T, but T can no longer sue L. As privity of estate now exists between L & A, A can sue L directly (and vice versa) on those covenants which "touch and concern" the land;

 (iii) If L then assigns the reversion to R, privity of estate now exists between R & A. There is neither privity of estate or privity of contract between R & T. Consequently only A and R can sue each other on any covenant which relates to the land;

 (iv) If A grants a subtenancy to ST and ST is in breach of a covenant in the headlease (the lease between L & T), there is no privity of estate nor contract between R & ST so R cannot sue ST directly. R will have to sue A and A will hope to pass liability on to ST.

4. Indemnity

In the light of the original landlord/tenant remaining liable for breaches of covenant by a future assignee, it is understandable that the original party can, in certain circumstances, claim indemnity from the true wrongdoer. The ways in which this can be achieved are:

  (a) in every assignment of the tenancy (but not the reversion) there is implied an indemnity covenant (s.77 of the LPA 1925) which entitles the original tenant to sue the assignee next in the chain, but no other assignee. This assignee will then pass responsibility down the chain and this process will continue until, hopefully, responsibility reaches the assignee at fault. Where there is a break in the chain (*e.g.* a former assignee is now dead) financial responsibility arbitrarily stops at the assignee next before the break;

  (b) as regards assignments of the landlord's reversion there is no implied covenant and an express covenant should be taken on each assignment. This is also so when a sub-tenancy is created when the sub-tenant should give his immediate landlord an express indemnity covenant;

(c) at common law, there exists a rule of common honesty which means that if, say, a tenant is under legal compulsion to pay an assignee's debts, the tenant can recover the money directly from the assignee in default: *Moule v Garrett* (1872).

Rules for Leases Created After 1995

The major criticism of the common law was the continuing liability of the original tenant throughout the lease and the potential liability of such tenants for breaches of covenant committed after an assignment of the lease had taken place. These injustices have, however, been tackled by the Landlord and Tenant (Covenants) Act 1995. The Act makes fundamental changes to the law affecting continuing liability both of tenants and landlords. This aspect of the Act applies only to tenancies created on or after January 1, 1996 and operates equally to legal and equitable leases.

1. The fundamental change is that an original tenant who assigns the lease is now automatically released from the burden of leasehold covenants: s.5. This will, in time, mark the end of continuing liability for original tenants. If only part of the property is assigned, the tenant will be released from any covenants that relate to that part. Where a covenant is not attributable to any part of the property that is being assigned then the landlord and tenant can enter into a contract as to the apportionment of liability: s.9.

2. The Act applies to both landlord covenants and tenant covenants whether or not they "touch and concern" land and whether the covenant is express, implied or imposed by law: ss.2,3. Personal obligations will not, however, be released on an assignment.

3. Although a tenant may cease to be liable on covenants after an assignment, the landlord may require a tenant who wishes to assign to give a guarantee for his *immediate* assignee by entering into an "authorised guarantee agreement". The assignor will, thereby, guarantee the performance of the covenants by his assignee (but no other): s.16. On a future assignment, the next assignor will give a new AGA. A guarantee may be insisted upon as a condition of the landlord giving consent to the proposed assignment. The authorised guarantee agreement may impose on the tenant:

(i) liability as sole or principal debtor of the assignee's obligations;

(ii) liability as a guarantor of the assignee providing the liabilities are not greater than those imposed on the assignee;

(iii) the obligation, if the tenancy is disclaimed by a trustee in bankruptcy, to take on any new lease for the duration of the term (this is sometimes called "a put-option").

4. Section 6 provides that an original landlord is not automatically released from his covenants on the assignment of the reversion. Under s.8, the landlord may serve a notice on the tenant informing him of the assignment and requesting release from the covenants. The release will be effective if the tenant consents or does not reply within the specified period or on the landlord's application to the court.

5. There are a number of situations where a landlord or tenant may not be released from their liability under agreed covenants. The effect of an excluded assignment is to defer the release of the tenant from liability to the next assignment which is not an excluded assignment: s.11. These "excluded assignments" are:

(i) assignments in breach of a covenant in the tenancy, *e.g.* an assignment in breach of a covenant against assignment, and

(ii) assignments by operation of law, *e.g.* an assignment on the death of a joint tenant of the legal estate;

6. The position of sub-tenants is unaffected by the 1995 Act, but in relation only to covenants which restrict the use of the premises a landlord can now enforce them directly against anyone in occupation (whether sub-tenant, licensee or trespasser): s.3(5).

Additional rules for leases whenever created

Certain provisions of the 1995 Act apply even where the lease was created before 1996:

1. Overriding lease. Where an original tenant or authorised guarantor has become liable for the acts of an assignee, and has made full payment in respect of that liability, he may call for an overriding lease. This will put him in the position of landlord to the defaulting assignee: s.19. The consequence of this is that the original tenant can deal with the property with a view to recovering some of the money paid out. It gives the original tenant control over the defaulting tenant, when he can sue for outstanding rent and potentially forfeiture of the lease with a view to re-letting.

2. Contractual variations. Under s.18, a former tenant or authorised guarantor will not be liable to pay any amount resulting from a variation of a covenant occurring after the assignment. This was, however, the position adopted at common law: *Beegas Nominees Ltd v BHP Petroleum Ltd* (1998). This does not apply to variations in rent following the original rent review machinery;

3. Fixed charges. Under s.17 the liability of a former tenant or authorised guarantor is limited in respect of any covenant under which a fixed charge is payable. There is no responsibility under the fixed charge covenant unless the landlord has served a notice, in the prescribed form, informing the former tenant/guarantor that any charge is due within six months of the date it becomes due. A fixed charge includes rent, service charges and liquidated sums for breach of covenant.

---

14. EXAMINATION CHECKLIST

1. How is property classified under English Law? Are leases treated as real or personal property?

2. What is land? In physical terms does land extend to the heavens above and down to the centre of the earth? If land is sold does it include fixtures and fittings? Note the tests the courts adopt to determine whether an item is a fixture or a fitting.

3. Explain the distinction between the doctrine of estates and the doctrine of tenures?

4. What type of estate am I dealing with? Is it freehold or leasehold; legal or equitable?

5. What restrictions exist on an "owner" of land? Examine the extent of these restrictions.

6. What is the nature of an equitable interest? What remedies are provided by equity and what is the significance of the doctrine of notice?

7. Does the estate or interest created fall within s.1 of the Law of Property Act 1925? Apply the section carefully to determine whether the estate or interest is capable of being legal.

8. If the estate has a condition attached to it, apply the required tests to determine whether it is a fee simple on condition subsequent or a determinable fee.

9. Examine the distinctions between a fee simple absolute in possession and a term of years absolute. Be able to analyse the meaning of each part of the statutory definitions.

10. What interests can be overreached and how does the overreaching machinery operate?

11. What interests can be protected by entry of a land charge? What are the consequences of registration and non-registration?

12. Explain the principles underpinning the system of registered conveyancing. Note the general effect of the Land Registration Act 2002 including the expansion of registrable rights and the reduction of overriding interests.

13. What is the meaning of "actual occupation" in the context of the Land Registration Act 2002? Be prepared to explain and develop the definition by reference to case law.

14. How are burdens/minor interests protected? Has the introduction of registered title impacted upon the doctrine of notice?

15. What is the effect of:

(a) a perpetually renewable lease;
(b) a lease for life; and
(c) a lease for an uncertain period?

16. Is exclusive possession essential for the creation of a lease? Be prepared to examine the case law and apply the tests adopted by the courts in recent cases. Explain the consequences of an agreement being construed as a licence rather than a lease.

17. How are leases created? Examine any formalities required and consider the conditions required to enforce a lease in equity.

18. Examine the express terms and conditions of the lease, together with any implied obligations, to determine the rights and duties of the landlord and tenant.

19. Has the tenant been responsible for any conduct that amounts to a breach of covenant that could give rise to forfeiture proceedings? Note the forfeiture procedures.

20. Examine the impact of the Trusts of Land and Appointment of Trustees Act 1996.

21. Does a co-ownership situation create a joint tenancy or a tenancy in common? Apply the following tests:

(a) Are the four unities present?
(b) What does the conveyance state?
(c) Are there any words of severance?
(d) Could any of the presumptions apply?

22. Has the joint tenancy been converted into a tenancy in common in equity? Make sure you are aware of how the joint tenancy can be severed, *e.g.* by sale, alienation, notice, unlawful killing, mutual agreement or by a course of conduct or dealing.
23. Where a trust of land arises who has the power of sale? What consultation, if any, needs to be made by the trustees?
24. Examine how a beneficial interest in co-owned property can arise by the use of a constructive trust. What role is now left for the resulting trust?
25. What rights can exist as easements? Give examples. Is the category of easements closed? You need to be familiar with the four essentials of an easement as laid down in *Re Ellenborough Park* (1956).
26. How was the easement created? Evaluate the methods of creation:

(a) Is there an express grant?
(b) Will the law imply an easement?
(c) Has there been long user sufficient to invoke the prescription provisions at common law, under the doctrine of Lost Modern Grant and/or under the Prescription Act 1832?

27. Ensure you understand the difference between an easement and *a profit à prendre*.
28. How is a mortgage created? Is the mortgage legal or equitable?
29. Examine the rights of the mortgagor and, in particular, the right to redeem (and any restrictions upon it).
30. How can a mortgagee protect his interest in the event of default by the mortgagor? Examine in detail the following powers of the mortgagee: sale, foreclosure, possession, appointment of a receiver and the right to sue on the personal covenant.
31. How are licences classified? Can a licence have a binding effect on a third party?
32. What criteria need to be satisfied for a proprietary estoppel to arise? Be prepared to examine how courts have satisfied the estoppel once any equity has been established.

33. Can the benefit and burden of positive and restrictive covenants be enforced?

   (a) at common law; and
   (b) in equity?

34. What rules govern the enforceability of covenants in leases? Note that the date the lease was created is of importance. Is the lease subject to the terms of the Landlord and Tenant (Covenants) Act 1995?

15. SAMPLE QUESTIONS AND MODEL ANSWERS

Question 1 (Co-ownership)

G, H, J, K and L, who are all of full age, bought a vacant plot of unregistered land known as "Parker's Piece" from N in 1994 hoping its value would increase. The conveyance, which the parties prepared without professional advice, was sealed by all the parties and purported to convey the land "to G, H, J, K and L as joint tenants in law and equity." The purchasers provided the purchase money equally.

In 1995 K died. In 1996 H purchased J's interest. In 1997 H died, appointing J as his executor. Recently L orally agreed to purchase G's interest in the property for £5,000.

Explain the devolution of the legal estate and of the equitable interests in "Parker's Piece," and advise L how he should protect his interest in the property.

Answer

The conveyance of the property to G, H, J, K and L creates a form of co-ownership, which is where land is conveyed to two or more persons simultaneously. Such co-ownership creates a trust of land under the provisions of the LPA 1925 and Trusts of Land and Appointment of Trustees Act 1996. The trustees of the co-owned property will hold the legal estate on a joint tenancy for the benefit of the equitable owners.

On January 1, 1997, the 1996 Act became operative. Consequently, the trust for sale was replaced with a trust of land under which the trustees have the powers of an absolute owner, subject to any express terms of the trust and exercisable consistent with the provisions of the Law of Property Act 1925 and 1996 Act.

The legal estate is held as an unseverable joint tenancy under the trust of land created by ss.34,36 LPA 1925 as amended by Part I of the 1996 Act.

If no trustees are specifically appointed, the first four individuals' named in the conveyance who are of full age and capacity will hold the legal estate as trustees. There can be no more than four trustees in this situation: s.36(1) of the LPA 1925; s.34 of the Trustee Act 1925, as amended. Consequently, G, H, J and K will hold the legal estate for the benefit of G, H, J, K and L in equity. In that the conveyance was prepared without professional advice and was sealed, this may operate as a valid deed provided it is also signed and witnessed.

The use of a trust simplifies conveyancing in that it enables a purchaser to deal only with the trustees and to effectively take free of the interests of the beneficiaries. The nature of a joint tenancy is that none of the parties are deemed to have separate rights as against the outside world. All they have is the potential right to the whole if they are the survivor. The *ius accrescendi* (right of survivorship) operates. It is no longer possible for the legal estate to be held on a tenancy in common.

In terms of the beneficial entitlement to the property it is necessary to decide whether the parties are joint tenants or tenants in common. Traditionally for a joint tenancy to exist the four unities must exist, *i.e.* unity of possession, title, time and interest. In that G, H, J, K and L acquire their rights by way of the 1994 conveyance this implies unity of title and time. They appear to have interests that are the same in extent, nature and duration, and the legal right to possession has been modified somewhat by ss.12,13 of the 1996 Act. Consequently the unities appear to be present, which is consistent with both a joint tenancy and a tenancy in common. It is only if one of the unities is missing that it can be concluded that a tenancy in common has been created. In that the conveyance provided that the parties were "joint tenants in law and equity" this will often be conclusive as to the status of the parties. The fact that the parties have provided the purchase money in equal shares is consistent with a joint tenancy. The fact that the parties bought the property hoping its value would increase would indicate a partnership venture, *i.e.* a common venture with a view to profit, and as the *ius accrescendi* has no place in business: *Lake v Craddock* (1732) this would be consistent with a tenancy in common. However, this is only a presumption and will bow to the evidence to the contrary in the conveyance with the conclusion that the parties are joint tenants in equity.

The effect of K's death in 1995 is that the legal estate will now be held by G, H and J as trustees. Because the legal estate is held on a joint tenancy the survivorship principle operates. As far as the beneficial interests are concerned again survivorship operates as the parties are joint tenants. The remaining parties G, H, J and L now have potential one-quarter shares instead of potential one-fifth shares.

When H purchases J's share this has no effect on the legal estate and J remains a trustee. The effect on the joint tenancy in equity is that severance takes place by way of the alienation of J's share to H. The unities of title and time are destroyed and, consequently, H holds a one-quarter share on a tenancy in common and the remaining three-quarters are still held on a joint-tenancy for G, H and L.

When H dies in 1997, the survivorship principle operates in respect of the legal estate and G and J hold the legal estate as trustees for the benefit of G and L as to three-quarters on a joint tenancy (H having lost his potential share by way of survivorship). The other one-quarter share on a tenancy in common which was held by H will now pass by virtue of his will to be held by his executor(s) for the benefit of his estate, the survivorship principle not operating in respect of a tenancy in common.

Recently L orally agreed to purchase G's interest in the property for £5,000. This has no effect on the legal estate, but raises the issues as to whether this can amount to a severance of the joint tenancy in equity. In that the agreement is oral, there cannot be a valid contract to transfer the share and, therefore, it cannot be treated as analienation. Similarly the oral agreement does not comply with s.36(2) LPA which provides that:

> ". . . where a legal estate (not being settled land) is vested in joint tenants beneficially and any tenant desires to sever the joint tenancy in equity, he shall give to the other joint tenants a notice in writing of such desire or do such other acts or things as would in the case of personal estate, have been effectual to sever the joint tenancy in equity."

Whilst the actions of L and G do not expressly come within s.36(2), it is in the nature of the "other acts and things" which incidentally are capable of effecting a severance as evidenced in *Re Drapers Conveyance* (1969) and in *Burgess v Rawnsley* (1975). There it was held that an oral agreement, in circumstances which clearly indicated that the parties treated themselves as having a share, amounted to a severance. Consequently the joint tenancy as to the three-quarters between G and L would appear to be severed and each party would be entitled to three-eighths of the purchase money. The final position would appear to be that the legal estate is held by G and J for the benefit of the estate of H as to one-quarter, and three-eighths for G and three-eighths for L (unless the agreement actually takes effect).

L not being a trustee should attempt to have himself appointed so that he may be able to take part in any management decision relating to the property. If L has the backing of the other beneficiaries, an application for appointment can be made under s.36 of the Trustee Act 1925 and ss.19,20 of the 1996 Act. Further, he should ensure that any severance of the joint tenancy is evidenced on the face of the conveyance so that, in the event of a single trustee dealing with the legal estate, a purchaser would have to insist on the appointment of a second trustee in accordance with the terms of the Law of Property (Joint Tenants) Act 1964.

Question 2 (Leasehold Covenats)

In 1990, K (the fee simple owner of a large agricultural estate) leased "The Briars", one of several houses on the estate, by deed to L for 21 years at a rent of £5000 per annum. The lease contained covenants by L to keep "The Briars" in good tenantable repair and to pay £25 per annum towards the upkeep of the private roads on K's estate. "The Briars" adjoins a public highway. L assigned the lease to M in 1992 and M assigned the lease to N in 1993. M has since been adjudged bankrupt. Explain to K how he can obtain damages from L or N, and who will be ultimately liable:

(a) if N allows "The Briars" to fall into disrepair; and
(b) if N refuses to contribute to the upkeep of the roads.

Answer

This question relates to the rules governing the enforceability of covenants between parties to a lease and their assignees.

Significant changes to this area of law have been made by the
Landlord and Tenant (Covenants) Act 1995 which became
operative on January 1, 1996. The majority of the provisions of
the Act are not retroactive and apply only to leases created after
the coming into force of the Act.

Given that the lease in the problem was granted in 1990 the
old common law rules will govern enforceability.

The relationship between K and L is one of privity of contract
in that they are the original landlord and tenant. The effect of
this is not only that K may enforce all the covenants in the lease
against L, whilst L retains the lease, but also that L remains
liable on the covenants for the whole term, notwithstanding any
assignment of the lease: *Warnford Investments Ltd v Duckworth*
(1979). It would of course have been open for K and L to restrict
their contractual obligations for the periods when they were
respectively to retain the lease or the reversion.

On the assignment of the lease to M, this creates a relationship
of privity of estate between K and M for the duration of the
period that M holds the lease. The consequence of privity of
estate is that the benefit and burden of all covenants that "touch
and concern" the land (*Spencers case* (1583)) or in the phraseol-
ogy of the ss.141,142 of the LPA, "have reference to the subject
matter of the lease", will pass with the land. Any covenant
which "affects the landlord in his capacity as landlord or the
tenant in his capacity as tenant" (Cheshire) may be said to touch
and concern the land. Any covenant which by its nature and not
merely through extraneous circumstances affect the nature,
quality or value of the land, or the mode of enjoying it, may fall
within the definition. Based on the decision in *Williams v Earle*
(1868), a covenant to repair property clearly touches and concerns the land and by analogy the burden of the covenant to
keep "The Briars" in good tenantable repair will pass with the
land. The covenant to contribute towards the upkeep of the
roads on the estate is less easy to classify in that we are told that
"The Briars" adjoins a public highway and, as a consequence,
any tenant may not use or have need of the private roads.
Covenants to pay rates in respect of other land: *Gower v
Postmaster-General* (1887) and to pay an annual sum to a third
person: *Mayho v Buckhurst* (1617) have been held not to touch
and concern the land on the ground that they did not affect the
land as such. An analogy may be drawn, but no definite
conclusion is possible. It must also be noted that for the rule in
Spencers case to operate the lease must be in due form, which

this one is, *i.e.* created by deed and there has to be a legal assignment of the whole term. The nature of the assignments are not specified in the question.

As between K and N there is privity of estate, N being the current tenant. This gives K a dual possibility in terms of his ability to sue. He can attempt to recover from L in privity of contract or sue N directly under privity of estate in respect of those covenants that have passed with the assignment, if any. L and N may both therefore be responsible for breach of the covenants but K can only obtain satisfaction from one, liability is alternative not cumulative: *City of London Corporation v Fell* (1994).

Since the lease is within the terms of the Leasehold Properties Repair Act 1938, K has a choice of remedy and in serving a section 146 notice may require forfeiture, although the question indicates that only damages are claimed.

In respect of the liability of L and N, primary liability is on the person causing the breach, namely N. As observed, K has the choice of suing either L or N. The liability of M would be restricted to any breaches caused by M during the period in which he held the lease, provided the burden of such covenants had passed.

If K chooses to sue L in privity of contract, a factor which may be motivated by the respective financial status of L and N, the issue of whether L can recover any damages he has to pay is raised. It is usual for an assignor to take a covenant of indemnity from the assignee, thereby guarding against future breaches of covenant. L may have taken such an indemnity from M, but we are specifically informed that M is bankrupt, in which case it may be difficult for M to satisfy any debt. In the absence of any express indemnity, s.77(1)(c) of the LPA 1925 implies an indemnity in any assignment for value, which may be the case here. This will not solve the problem of M's bankruptcy and an alternative method enabling L to sue N direct needs to be found. The solution would appear to arise under the rule in *Moule v Garrett* (1872), which on restitutionary principles enables a joint debtor, who has paid money to a common creditor for the exclusive benefit of the other co-debtor, to recover direct from that person. Consequently if L pays damages to K in respect of any breach for which N is responsible then by application of this principle L can recover direct from N and need not sue through the chain involving M: *Re Healing Research Trustee Co.* (1992). Where the burden of any covenant has not passed with the assignment then L will be liable for damages and will have no method of recovery.

Note: had the lease in the problem been created after 1995 then the terms of the 1995 Act would have applied in full. The major change affecting the problem being that the original covenantor would be liable in respect of leasehold covenants (not personal ones) only when the lease was vested in him. This effectively releases any tenant from liability after assignment (Ch.13 deals with the new changes in full).

Question 3 (Estates and Leases)

Consider the effect of the following limitations in a deed taking effect today:

(a) to A for one year with an option to renew on the same terms;

(b) to B for 21 years or until his death, whichever is the earlier;

(c) to C for 21 years, to commence when C marries.

Answer

(a)   The grant of the property for one year by deed would create a legal term of years absolute within s.1(1) of the LPA 1925, *i.e.* it is a legal lease for one year initially. The reference to the option to renew on the same term raises the question as to whether this creates a perpetually renewable lease. In order for such a lease to exist there has to be a reference to the renewal clause itself, though this has not always been the case as is highlighted by decisions such as *Parkus v Greenwood* (1950) and *Northchurch Estates Ltd v Daniels* (1947). In the latter of these cases, an option to renew "on identical terms and conditions" was held to create a perpetually renewable lease. The current view is that the courts lean against the interpretation of a perpetually renewable lease unless there is a specific reference to the renewal clause itself. This is illustrated by the decision in *Burnett v Barclay* (1980). Consequently, as there is no specific reference here to the existence of the renewal clause, the better view is that this is a single renewal only. Had it been a perpetually renewable lease it would have converted to a term of 2,000 years under the LPA 1922, s.145, and Schedule 15.

A single option to renew is an estate contract and as such is registrable under the Land Charges Act 1972, and must be registered in order to be enforceable against any subsequent purchaser for money or monies worth of the legal estate. The effect of the limitation is, therefore, that A can occupy the property for one year initially with a renewal for a single year.

(b) For a lease to create a legal term of years absolute within LPA 1925, s.1(1), it must be created in the correct manner (*i.e.* by deed, unless it falls within the three-year oral exception created by LPA, s.54(2)). For any lease to exist, exclusive possession must be given together with the fact that there is certainty of duration. Here a lease is granted for 21 years, but is determinable on the dropping of a life. If the lease is at a rent or fine it may fall within LPA 1925, s.149(6), as "... a term of years determinable with life or lives ..." and, as such, would be converted into a 90-year term: *Skipton B.S. v Clayton* (1993). If no rent or fine is paid and the lease is gratuitous the section will not apply and the lease will operate as a term for 21 years determinable on B's death. Such a lease cannot be legal as it contravenes the meaning of "absolute" in s. 205(1) of the LPA 1925 in that it is determinable on the dropping of a life. Consequently it would be an equitable lease only.

(c) As a pre-requisite of any valid lease there has to be certainty of duration, *i.e.* the maximum duration of the term must be calculable. The problem here is that the lease is to commence on an uncertain event, although once it commences there is certainty of duration. An analogy can be drawn with *Askew v Tarmac Roadstone Holdings* (1991), where a lease containing a commencement date by reference to the date of a planning permission at some future date was held to be too uncertain. It should also be noted that a lease must not contravene the LPA 1925, s.149(3), which provides that a lease at a rent limited to take effect more than 21 years from the date of the instrument creating it is void. The question creates the basic problem of uncertainty as to when C marries. If a term of years is fixed by reference to some collateral matter, such matter must either be itself certain or capable of becoming certain before the lease takes effect: *Lace v Chantler* (1944). Consequently, it may be argued that as it is uncertain when the marriage will take place the lease is void.

Question 4 (Mortgages—Power of Sale of the Mortgagee)

In 1997 Hugh borrowed £5,000 from Jack secured by a first legal mortgage of Hugh's unregistered freehold house, Whiteacre. In

October 1998 Hugh borrowed a further £3,000 with interest at 12
per cent from Pam secured by a second legal mortgage on
Whiteacre. Hugh has now fallen into arrears with his payments
of interest due under the second mortgage. Jack holds the title
deeds of Whiteacre.

(a) Explain in what circumstances Pam could sell Whiteacre
to secure repayment of her loan and how any such sale
would affect Jack's position.
(b) If in the exercise of any power of sale she may have Pam
sells Whiteacre at less than its open market value, would
Hugh have any remedy against:
(i) Pam, or
(ii) the purchaser from Pam?
(c) How must Pam apply the proceeds of any such sale of
Whiteacre and what special precautions must she take in
doing so?

Answer

(a) A power of sale arises in accordance with LPA 1925, s.101,
if the mortgage has been made by deed and the mortgage
money is due (provided no contrary intention is shown in the
deed). If the mortgage is to be paid by instalment this arises as
soon as any instalment is in arrears. The power of sale is
exercisable under the terms of LPA, s.103, when one of three
conditions is satisfied, namely that some interest under the
mortgage is at least two months in arrears; that there has been
three months' default in repayment of the loan after notice
requiring it has been served on the mortgagor; or that there has
been a breach of some provision in the LPA 1925 or some
covenant in the mortgage deed (other than for repayment of
mortgage money or interest). It should, however, be noted that
these statutory powers may be varied or extended by the
mortgage deed. The question does not indicate the extent of the
arrears in the payment of interest under Pam's mortgage, but if
that interest is at least two months in arrears, the power of sale
has become exercisable. The mortgage is legal and s.101 consequently appears to have been complied with (the legal redemption date often being six months after the creation of the
mortgage).

As to Jack's position being a prior mortgagee any sale by Pam
is subject to his mortgage: LPA, s.104(1), and on a sale he can

elect to have his mortgage paid from the proceeds of sale, or alternatively the sale of the property will remain incumbranced by his mortgage.

(b) Pam is not a trustee for the mortgagor, but must act in good faith, however there is no obligation on her to sell by auction or to advertise the property. As a general rule sale at a low price will not be interfered with in the absence of fraud or negligence. If a sale takes place at less than the open market value this raises an inference of lack of good faith and damages may be awarded. In *Cuckmere Brick Co. Ltd v Mutual Finance Ltd* (1971) where damages were awarded to compensate for a sale of a plot of land where full particulars had not been given, it was stated by Salmon L.J. that ". . . a mortgagee in exercising his power of sale owes a duty to take reasonable precautions to obtain the true market value of the mortgaged property on the date on which he decides to sell." In *Bank of Cyprus v Gill* (1979), it was suggested that the mortgagee must get the best available price, but this may be overstating the case and, indeed, in *Downsview Nominees Ltd v First City Corp.* (1992) the court doubted whether a mortgagee on sale had any duty of care in negligence to later incumbrancers or the mortgagor himself when exercising the power. If Hugh agrees with Pam that the property can be sold at less than the market price, Hugh would be estopped from relying on any duty of care that may exist provided there was no evidence of undue or unconscionable action on Pam's part: *Mercantile Credit Co. v Clarke* (1997). If Pam fails to observe any required duty in exercising the sale and sells at an artificially low price, then damages may be payable to Hugh. In *Tomlin v Lace* (1889), where a mortgagee had mis-described the property he had to make an allowance to the purchaser from the price and was held liable to the mortgagor for the difference.

Pam could not sell the property to herself either directly or through an agent as this would not be a bona fide sale: *Tse Kwong Lam v Wong Chit Sen* (1983).

(c) Once the power of sale has arisen (s.101) the mortgagee can give a good title to the purchaser free from the equity of redemption, even if the power of sale has not become exercisable: s.104. If the purchaser is aware of any facts showing that the power of sale has not become exercisable or that there is any impropriety in the sale, he will not get a good title.

Consequently, any purchaser from Pam would obtain a good title provided he was not aware that the sale was abnormally low or that there was any fraud, bad faith or impropriety involved.

(d)   Pam must pay off the prior mortgage of Jack (if this is agreed) and apply the remainder of the proceeds of sale in accordance with s.105 which makes Pam a trustee of those proceeds to be applied in the following order:

  (i) to pay the expenses of the sale;
 (ii) to pay the principal sum, interest and costs of the selling mortgagee's loan;
(iii) to pay the residue to the next incumbrancer, but if none then what remains is to be paid to the mortgagor.

Pam must make sure that in paying over the residue it is to the person best entitled. She should check in the relevant register to determine whether any later mortgages have been registered, and if so this amounts to notice to her. If she pays the residue to Hugh without making this inquiry and it transpires that subsequent mortgagees exist there will be liability.

INDEX